Paper-Cutting Stories
for
Holidays and Special Events

By Valerie Marsh

Illustrated by Patrick K. Luzadder

Alleyside Press

Fort Atkinson, Wisconsin

To Matt, Marie, Renee, Celeste, and Weston
who love holidays and celebrations

Also written by Valerie Marsh:
Paper-Cutting Stories from A to Z
Mystery-Fold: Stories to Tell, Draw, and Fold

Published by Alleyside Press, an imprint of Highsmith Press

Highsmith Press
W5527 Highway 106
P.O. Box 800
Fort Atkinson, Wisconsin 53538-0800

1-800-558-2110

The paper used in this publication meets the minimum requirements of
American National Standard for Information Science —
Permanence of Paper for Printed Library Material. ANSI/NISO Z39.48-1992.

Library of Congress Cataloging in Publication

Marsh, Valerie.
    Paper-cutting stories for holidays and special events / by Valerie
Marsh.
        p.   cm.
    ISBN 0-917846-42-7 (alk. paper)
    1. Holidays. 2. Special days. 3. Storytelling. 4. Paper work.
5. Creative activities and seat work. I. Title.
GT3930.M37 1994
394.2'6--dc20   94-26174

Contents

Introduction 5

January

Sammy's Special Present ★
Birthday 9

The Anchor ★
New Year's Day 11

February

Gifts from the Heart
Valentine's Day 14

Not Just Peanuts
Black History Month 16

March

A Lucky Catch
St. Patrick's Day 19

The First Woman Doctor
Women's History Month 21

April

Earth Day Dolphins
Earth Day 23

The Tooth-Picking Giants
Arbor Day 26

May

Cinco de Mayo
Mexican Heritage 30

A New Flag ★
Memorial Day 32

June

Not Just Another Tie
Father's Day   36

July

The Liberty Bell
Fourth of July   39

August

I Don't Want to Go
Back to School   42

September

Two Packages
Grandparent's Day   44

October

Cabin Girl
Columbus Day   47

A Revolutionary Ghost Story ★
Halloween   50

November

Turkey Feathers
Thanksgiving   53

December

Cookie Cutters
Hanakkah   56

**The Christmas Angel &
The First Christmas Tree**
Christmas   59

Kwanzaa
Kwanzaa   62

(★These stories can be used during other months.)

Introduction

Why storytelling?

Storytelling is *fun*! Fun for the listeners and the teller!

The best way to tell a great story is to be a storyteacher, not a storyteller! As a storyteacher you are not telling stories for entertainment, but to demonstrate to children how they themselves can tell stories. This takes the pressure off of you to be a great performer. Instead, you are just doing what you probably do everyday and that is—work with children. When you think of it in this context, storytelling becomes easy. You are a storyteacher. Storyteaching has one main goal and that is to empower children to tell stories.

Just by listening to your story, children develop many higher level thinking skills. These include the skills of critical thinking, short- and long-term memory, analysis, synthesis, sequencing and most importantly—creative imagination! Children learn to distinguish between reality and fantasy. They gain in general knowledge, compassion and self-confidence.

Using scissors and cutting paper helps develop fine motor and motor planning skills. And finally, while listening to a story we all can escape from the real world for a few moments and come back to it with renewed vigor and increased confidence.

These stories are for children ages three to 12. Obviously, a ten-year-old listener brings different experiences and expectations to the story than does a three-year-old. But each listener gains what he needs to from your story at that particular moment in his life.

One thing that storyteachers need to remember is to repeat favorite stories. Sometimes in the repeating a story will become a favorite. Every story deserves to be told at least twice. A child's requests for a particular story should be honored whenever possible.

What is paper-cutting?

Folding and cutting the "answer" to a story out of a piece of paper is a unique way to tell a story, and it yields an unusual surprise for the listener. It is also a great way for children to learn to tell stories. The stories in this book are short, easy to tell and deceptively simple. The stories and their corresponding cut-out pictures are designed to be simple enough for school-age children to retell or revise into their own versions. They can simply be enjoyed by very young children.

As you tell these stories, you will be cutting an object out of a folded piece of construction paper. At the end of the story, the object is completely cut out and unfolded. The paper-cutting object is an integral part of the story.

After you tell a few of these stories, your students will soon be telling their own paper-cutting tales both at home and at school. Some children will bring stories to school that they have made up at home; this generates enthusiasm in other children to do the same thing. Before you know it, parents will also be involved, looking forward to hearing the paper-cutting stories their children learn at school. They can even help their child create new stories!

Why combine storytelling and paper-cutting?

Telling a story while cutting a piece of paper is a great way to completely capture your listeners' interest. This is an unusual approach to storytelling and when you end with an object that is key to the story—Wow!—you've got a really memorable story!

Watching the object emerge from the paper helps both the storyteller and the listeners remember the steps of the story. The cutting lines are related to the plot, and the object created is important to the outcome of your story.

Another plus: When speaking in front of a group, most people feel more confident if they have something to do with their hands; the paper and scissors fulfill this need.

Most children love to cut and spend lots of time at it. After experiencing a paper-cutting story involving a simple object, children will often take their own ideas and turn them into a story.

Do you need to be an artist or seasoned storyteller?

No! All you need to do is trace! These patterns are designed to be used with typing paper. You do not have to cut freehand; all lines are traced lightly before telling the story. You can also use a larger size paper. Remember—you are a storyteacher—telling a story in order to teach children how to tell stories.

When should you tell paper-cutting stories?

Holiday Parties—Choose a paper-cutting story to match the holiday.

Birthdays—Tell "Sammy's Special Present," changing the name to that of the birthday person.

Rewards—Children need to learn that rewards can take forms other than material things such as food, stickers, etc. Rewards can also be active entertainment rather than passive (such as a movie).

Quiet times after recess.

Waiting times between classes or during lunch periods.

Unexpected delays such as waiting for a late speaker during a school convocation.

Entertainment at a school fair or carnival.

After-school art and crafts programs.

After-school child-care programs.

Curriculum integration of art, listening skills, sequencing skills, writing skills, history.

How to tell Paper-Cutting stories

1. First place a piece of white paper over the pattern in the book. With a pencil, trace all cutting lines lightly. Fold where indicated. If you are using white paper to tell your story, you are ready to go. If you want to transfer the cutting lines to colored paper, then cut out your white pattern, place it on the colored paper and trace around it.

2. Practice telling your story while cutting so that it becomes natural to talk and draw at the same time. Cutting steps are related to the story. As the character goes places or does something, you cut a new line. Becoming familiar with the story and the cutting allows you to present the story easily and develop a natural rapport with your listeners. When you are not cutting, just hold the paper and scissors naturally or put them down if you need to use your hands to talk.

   If you forget what comes next or get stuck in a story, ask the youngsters to repeat what's happened thus far (giving you time to think) of suggest what could come next.

3. Retell the story at least once. Retelling the story gives the listener a second chance to enjoy it as well as to learn the story and the cutting steps. Stories can and should be changed by each storyteller, and a story will be a little bit different each time it is told.

4. There are countless variations of paper-cutting. You can fold a differently colored paper inside as in "Not Just Peanuts." You can fold the paper into quarters, as in "The Anchor," or "Revolutionary Ghost Story." The paper does not even have to be folded—just cut out an object as you tell a story, as in "Kwanzaa." You can color any part of the object before, during

or after the telling. The "Kwanzaa" story is very effective if you color the candles before cutting. You and your students will surprise yourselves at how creative you can be with the paper-cutting concept.

How you and your students can create original paper-cutting stories

1. Decide on a story to tell, then choose something to paper-cut that is an integral part of the story. Or first choose an object to cut, then find a story or write a story involving that holiday or object. Objects should be symmetrical. "How to draw" books (available in most libraries) are a great resource for ideas.

2. Prefold your paper and draw one half of your object against the folded side lightly with a pencil. Practice telling your story, relating the cutting steps to the storyline. As a character goes places or does things, make your next cut.

3. This is a great time to teach story elements. Every story needs the following:

   a. an introduction
   b. characters
   c. location or setting
   d. action or plot
   e. resolution or good ending

4. Expect simple, imperfect cut-outs and stories from your listeners. Their stories might even be remarkably similar to one that you have just told. That is okay and quite a compliment to you. You might need to encourage a reluctant child who "just can't think of anything." Help him draw a picture to cut out from one printed on his shirt, his notebook or hung on a classroom bulletin board. Get the child started by asking questions such as, "What else does this outline of a snowman make you think of? Does it look like a path? Are some kids walking down this path (indicate outline of snowman) when they get lost?"

5. Plan to have several sheets of paper for each student. Encourage them to practice telling their story to themselves first and then to a friend. It is also a good idea to have them write their story down. When they tell it to you, you can help them perfect it.

6. After several practices with small groups over a period of several days, your storytellers will be ready to present their story to the rest of the group. After their presentation, you might want to reward each child with a "Storytelling Certificate" or another story told by you.

To guarantee your success

Using your imagination, you can come up with all kinds of stories and ways to paper-cut. A few simple tips guarantee a pleasurable, successful story session every time:

• Select an appropriate story for your listeners.

• Prefold your paper.

• Trace lightly over all cutting lines on your paper.

• Be familiar with the story. You can make notes to yourself on the paper that you will be cutting.

• Be ready (with additional sheets of prepared paper) to tell your paper-cutting story several times. You will hear, "Tell it again!"

• Have in mind some ideas for discussion after you tell the story.

• Have paper and scissors ready for your listeners if you plan on asking them to participate.

• Enjoy yourself!

CELEBRATE WITH A STORY!!!!

1

Sammy's Special Present

Sammy was so excited. He was going to his friend Dudley's birthday party. He and his mom had made a very special birthday present for Dudley, and Sammy was excited about giving it to him. His mother had told him the way to Dudley's house: "Walk down our street to the end. Turn left and go around the corner. Dudley lives on Brentwood Street. You'll know his house because he'll have a big bunch of balloons tied to his mailbox. And remember—carry the present very carefully and don't drop it." Sammy said, "Okay, Mom. I can find his house and I won't drop his present." Sammy started walking down his street. *(Cut from #1 to #2.)*

He turned left. *(Cut from #2 to #3.)* But when he got around the corner, he wasn't sure which street was Dudley's. Was it this first one? He started walking down this street. It turned into a dead end, and he didn't see any mailboxes with balloons. *(Cut from #3 to #4 to #5.)*

So Sammy decided to try the next street. Maybe this would be Dudley's street. He walked down the street. It also turned into a dead end, and there were no balloons anywhere! *(Cut from #6 to #7 to #8.)* Well, maybe it was the next one. He was sure to find it soon. *(Repeat this step as many times as desired. If you are telling this story to a particular grade level or child, you might want to have Sammy walk down half as many streets as the children are old.)*

Soon, Sammy came to the last street in the neighborhood. Dudley's house had to be on this street! He started walking down the street. Was that a mailbox over there with balloons on it? Yes, it was! *(Cut from #9 to #10 to #11.)*

Sammy ran up Dudley's sidewalk just as Dudley opened the door. *(Cut from #11 to #12.)*

"Happy Birthday, Dudley!"

"Thanks, Sammy, I'm six years old today!"

"I know, Dudley. My mom and I made you a special birthday present. Here it is! Happy Birthday!" *(Open up the folded paper and show the cake to the listeners.)*

Today we are celebrating _____'s birthday. We wish you a happy birthday _____. Here is _____ birthday cake. Is this how old you are? *(Indicate candles on cut-out cake. Discuss how you could cut out the candles if the birthday person was an odd number of years old.)*

Note: You might want to change the names in this story to those of the birthday child and one of his/her friends.

Fold Line

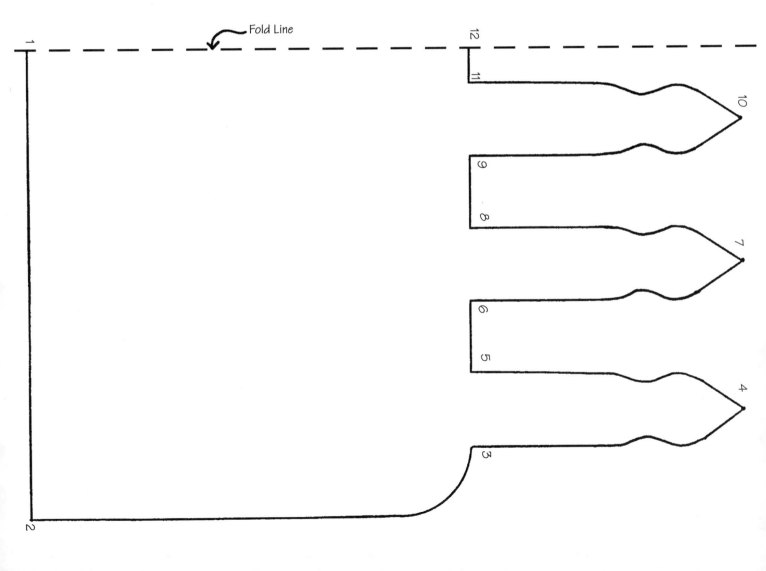

2
The Anchor

The storm came up suddenly and even though Dave had done all the right things, his boat was in danger of crashing onto the reef. He picked up his anchor, and threw it overboard to keep the boat from being smashed against the rocks. *(Cut from #1 to #2.)* Just then several great waves roared at him, and he was thrown out of the boat. Desperately swimming toward shore, he was washed onto some rocks, where he also found the boat's anchor and rope. The waves smashing onto the rocks were so strong that he was barely able to tie the rope around his waist.

Throughout the storm, the anchor kept him from being washed back into the ocean. Dave spent the night wet, cold and worried—more worried about his very pregnant wife Linda than about himself.

When Dave arrived home, all he was carrying was his anchor. *(Cut from #3 to #4.)*

"Dave! Oh, thank goodness, you're all right. We knew you got caught in that sudden storm. We were worried sick about you!" exclaimed his sister.

"How's Linda? Has the baby been born yet?" asked Dave anxiously.

"Oh yes! Come and see!"

"Linda, how are you! Our baby! Oh, how beautiful he? she? is!"

"It's a girl, Dave! Shall we call her Jenni as we planned?"

"Definitely! And I have a present for her—her first one!" Dave lugged in the anchor. *(Cut from #5 to #6.)*

"An anchor? Why, that's the one from your fishing boat!" exclaimed Linda.

"This anchor saved my life, Linda. It held me safe and secure during that terrible storm. I'm sure our love for Jenni will hold her safe and secure. I'm lucky to be alive, and this is definitely a lucky anchor. Let's keep it in her bedroom."

As Jenni grew, she developed a love for the sea, spending much of her time just watching the boats and the fishermen. She counted all of the fishermen as her friends, but there was one she was particularly fond of. Well, he wasn't exactly a fisherman, but he did go out in his boat everyday. His name was John, and he was a history professor from the community college. One day Jenni saw him down at the beach.

"Why are you so sad, John?" asked Jenni.

"Jenni, this is my last day here. I'm out of money. I've spent all this time looking for the wreck of the Aletania and I still haven't found it. I guess that part of our history will be lost forever."

"Oh, John, I'm so sorry." Jenni thought for a minute. "Hey, I've got an idea! Stay here! Just stay here and I'll be right back! Don't move! I know just what you need!"

Jenni ran back home and picked up her lucky anchor. She slowly lugged it back to the dock. "Here John! Use this! It will help you.!"

"What is this? An anchor!" asked John.

"John, this is not just *any* anchor! It is my lucky anchor! It saved my dad's life the night I was born. It's always kept me lucky. I know it will bring you luck too."

"Thanks, Jenni. I'll use it right now. I have nothing to lose—it *is* my last trip out."

Late that night, there was a banging on their door. Dave answered it with Jenni right behind her dad. "John, what are you doing here?"

11

"I found it! I found the wreck of the Aletania and it's all because of the lucky anchor! I just know those diamonds went down with the ship."

"What? What are you talking about!?" asked Dave.

John explained, "Jenni gave me her lucky anchor this afternoon. I cast it out on my last trip to the reef. I drifted awhile before the anchor caught. I wasn't in the right area according to the histories of the wreck and my studies of the maps. But it *was* the spot, because when I pulled the anchor back up, a cannon ring had gotten hooked on it. It had the Aletania's markings on it! Here's hoping we can now learn more about the early sailors and find those famous diamonds that sunk! It looks like I'm here to stay for awhile. Here's your lucky anchor back! Thanks a lot!"

"You keep it, John," piped up Jenni, "and give it to the next person who really needs some good luck."

"Are you sure? OK, I will. That's a good idea. Thanks!" said John.

You know, that good-luck anchor was passed around that little fishing village for many, many years. In fact, it even ended up back in Dave, Linda and Jenni's family once or twice. You might say it created a circle of good will; of people wishing each other good fortune and happiness. *(Open up anchor to show circle.)* And that's a really good wish to give each other at the beginning of each new year—Good Fortune and Happiness!

Happy New Year!

Note: You can use this story for another holiday. Just change the last sentence of the story to go with your holiday. For example: "And that's a really good wish to give each other on The First Day of Spring, Valentine's Day, etc."

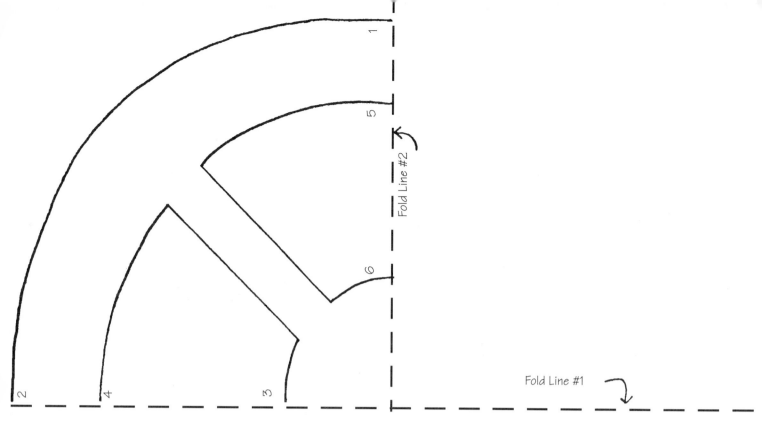

1

5

6

Fold Line #2

2

4

3

Fold Line #1

Cut Line: The circle needs to be cut from a square, so cut this section off before folding.

"THE ANCHOR"

Cut brown or gray paper into a square, then fold in half.

Fold again into quarters before cutting.

3
Gifts from the Heart

Here's a short Valentine story that you can do with me. I'll tell it first and then we'll tell it again together.

Once there was a little kid who loved making things with paper. He learned how to make a square. He folded one corner of a piece of typing paper across to the other side and then cut off the remaining strip. *(Fold corner over, cut off strip.)* That gave him a square.

Then this little kid, Josh, opened up the paper and folded it in half. Now he had a rectangle. *(Fold in half.)*

Josh asked, "What can I make with a rectangle? I want something for Valentine's Day. Well, how about if I make this into a square? What could I do with that? *(Fold your paper into a square.)* I'm not sure what a person can make from a square for Valentine's Day."

"Maybe I should turn this into a triangle," said Josh. *(Fold square into a triangle.)*

Josh looked at this triangle for a minute. "What can this be? A hat? *(Put it on your head.)* A duck's beak? *(Open and close it in front of your mouth.)* I think I'll trim it a little." *(Cut curve line #1.)*

"What does it look like now?" thought Josh. *(Elicit suggestions from listeners.)* "Yes, this does remind me of an ice cream cone! Hey, that gives me an idea! I think I'll make one for my little brother and me for Valentine's Day."

(Open out to heart.) "What is this? *(Pause.)* Yes! A heart! I've got another good idea. You know my sister would enjoy a nice heart-shaped box of chocolates for Valentine's Day," said Josh.

(Open out next lobe so that you now have three lobes. Fan your face with it.) What does this remind you of? Yes, that's exactly what Josh thought it was—a fan!

"Now that's a great idea! I could give my mom one of those fancy fans they sell at the dollar store. She'd like that for Valentine's Day."

(Open out to four lobes.) "OK, what about this? You know what this reminds me of? Yes, a roller coaster! *(Trace finger over each curve.)* So now I know what I can give my dad. I'll write him a coupon that says I'll be glad to go with him this summer to the amusement park. What a great Valentine's Day gift!"

(Open up paper completely.) "And here is a—flower! I can give my grandmother some flowers for Valentine's Day. She loves flowers. Now I have a gift for everyone in my family: a flower for Grandma, a roller coaster ride for Dad, a fan for Mom, a box of chocolate for my sister and an ice cream cone for my little brother! What a neat Valentine's Day we will have!" *(Refold paper as you mention each gift.)*

Happy Valentine's Day!

Hand out paper and scissors to listeners and let them retell it with you. Encourage the children to come up with other ideas for Valentine gifts. Using crayons or markers, turn the hearts into pictures of animals, designs or the objects mentioned in the story.

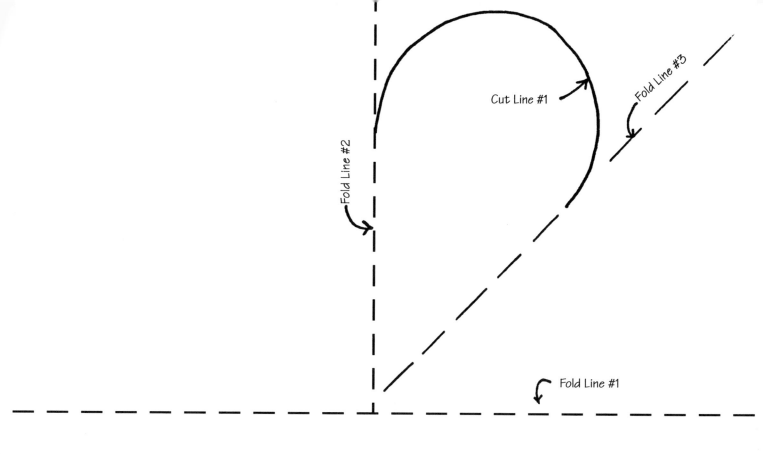

Fold Line #2

Cut Line #1

Fold Line #3

Fold Line #1

Cut Line

"GIFTS FROM THE HEART"
Cut paper into square at cut line.
Fold square paper in half at line #1.
Fold paper again at fold line #2.
Fold paper into triangle at fold line #3.
Use red, pink, purple or lavender paper.

4

Not Just Peanuts

Goober is an old, old African word for peanut. Africans on slave ships ate boiled goobers twice a day. Some slaves who ended up in Virginia planted goobers at the sides of their cabins. Peanuts were a great food in their diet. Soon most farms and plantations in the South had little goober gardens. Everyone liked munching on goobers.

This is the story of a man who discovered more than 300 uses for the goober. His name was George Washington Carver.

George Washington Carver was born just when slavery was ending. Slave babies took the last name of the family who owned them. George's mother, Mary, was the only slave the Carver family owned. After George's mother died, Susan Carver raised George and his older brother, Jim, as her own children.

George Carver wanted to go to school but there were no schools for African American children near the Carver farm, so Susan Carver taught George his letters and numbers. When George was 12, he walked eight miles to the nearest town that did have a school. *(Cut from #1 to #2.)* When he finally arrived, he was so tired that he lay down in a barn next to the school and fell fast asleep.

When he woke up the next morning the first thing he saw was an African American woman hanging out laundry in the barnyard. It was Mariah Watkins. She and her husband Andrew didn't have any children of their own and they invited George Carver to live with them while he attended school next door. When he wasn't in school, George helped Mariah with the laundry she did for other people. George loved reading so much that he propped up a book in front of the laundry tub so he could study while scrubbing the clothes. *(Cut from*

#2 to #3 and show laundry tub.) The books he really liked best were about plants. He loved to study about plants and how they grew and reproduced.

When George Carver had learned everything he could at the Lincoln School, he knew he needed to move on. So at age 16, he got a ride in a wagon with a family traveling to Kansas. There he got a job as a cook. He saved all his money to pay for books and schooling. Then George Carver was taken in by another childless couple, the Seymours. Lucy Seymour was a laundress just like Mariah Watkins. So George Carver knew exactly how to help her. Eventually George Carver set up his own laundry business in a small shack in Minneapolis. It was soon filled with George's plants and friends.

There were two George Carvers in town and they often received each other's mail. George Carver decided to solve the problem by adding a "W" to the middle of his name. "The 'W' stands for Washington," he said proudly. "I am George Washington Carver."

In 1890, when George Washington Carver was 26 years old, he finally achieved his life-long dream—attending college. He had washed a lot of clothes in laundry tubs to get there. *(Finish cutting out laundry tub, and hold up white side only.)*

In college he studied his favorite subject, botany, or the science of plants, and soon became a professor for his college. One day he received a request from Booker T. Washington, who invited him to come and be a teacher at his school, Tuskegee Institute in Alabama.

George Washington Carver remembered all the tubs of laundry that he had scrubbed in order to get his schooling. *(**Indicate laundry tub.**)* He wanted to help other African Americans. He decided to go.

At Tuskegee, Carver showed his students how to make fertilizer, and how to plant a variety of crops, not just cotton. He tried to convince them that the soil needed a chance to rest after all those years of growing nothing but cotton.

George Washington Carver also helped educate the local farmers on how to improve their farming methods.

In the early 1900s, the cotton crop was not doing well. George Washington Carver advised everyone to plant goobers or peanuts. But then the farmers had more peanuts than they could sell. They went to Carver and said, "You told us to plant peanuts and so we did. Look at all of them! So many peanuts! Now what do we do with them all!?"

Carver locked himself in his laboratory for several months doing research and working with the goobers. He discovered lots of other things to do with too many peanuts, besides eating them. He found peanuts could be made into cooking oil, margarine, shoe polish, and of course, peanut butter!

George Washington Carver's life was one about caring and giving. He worked hard early in his life washing laundry in a tub, *(**indicate tub**)* and later on helping farmers and discovering many uses for peanuts. *(**Turn paper over to show a peanut cut from brown paper.**)* He dedicated his life to helping others.

George Washington Carver is one of the great African Americans we remember during this Black History Month.

Happy Black History Month!

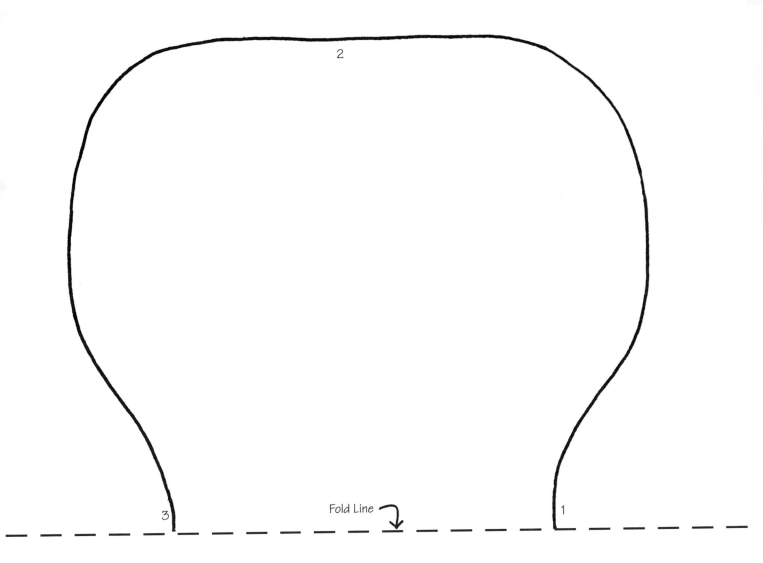

2

3

Fold Line ⤵

1

"NOT JUST PEANUTS"

Before starting the story,
place brown or beige paper
under white paper and fold
both in half so that only
white shows.

5
A Lucky Catch

The Saint Patrick's Day Fishing Contest was set for tomorrow. Kevin loved to fish and he was good at it. He really wanted to catch the biggest fish and win the cash prize. Things hadn't been going too well lately with his farm and the prize money would help buy food for his young family. Counting on the luck of the Irish to help him win, Kevin picked several small plants from his farm field to take with him to the fishing contest. *(Cut from #1 to #2.)*

Fortunately, it turned out to be a nice day.

Unfortunately, all the good fishing spots were taken by the time Kevin got out on the lake.

Fortunately, he found one spot left.

Unfortunately, it was the worst spot.

Fortunately, he hooked something right away. *(Cut from #2 to #3.)*

Unfortunately, it was not a fish but an old boot that he pulled out of the water. How embarrassing—to hook a boot at the most important fishing contest of the year.

Fortunately, he was able to hide it in the bottom of his boat before his friends saw it.

Unfortunately, Kevin did have to get rid of it somehow. He couldn't just throw it back into the water. Someone might see him.

Fortunately, as Kevin walked back home with the boot wrapped up in his scarf he saw a ravine, a valley with hills on both sides. Kevin threw the boot with all his might into the ravine.

Unfortunately, his scarf caught on the boot as he wound up to throw. When he threw the boot, his scarf went with it. Now he had to climb down and get it. *(Cut from #3 to #4.)*

Fortunately, it was pretty easy to climb down.

Unfortunately, when he got down to the bottom of the ravine, he saw that his scarf was tangled up in a sticker bush. Now Kevin had to spend time untangling it.

Fortunately, just as he got his scarf loose, he saw something lying under the bush. Kevin picked it up—and you know—it was a key. *(Cut from #4 to #5.)*

Unfortunately, all the way home, he couldn't think of anything that this key would unlock. It was a rather unusual looking key.

Fortunately, Kevin's wife didn't even notice that he was late, and she forgot to ask about the fishing contest.

Unfortunately, she never did like old antique things, and she told him to get rid of the key.

Fortunately, Kevin took the key to McClarney's Antique Shop. *(Cut from #6 to #7.)*

His friend Patrick, the owner of the shop, bought the key from him. He paid Kevin more money than he would have won at the fishing contest. That is because this particular key was a very rare key. Turns out that old boot was a pretty lucky catch! *(Cut from #7 to #8. Open out string of Shamrocks.)*

Those small leafy plants from his farm field had brought Kevin the best luck imaginable.

(Unfold paper.) Do you know what these are? That's right—these are shamrocks!

Happy St. Patrick's Day!

Before telling: Accordion fold a 4 1/2" by 18" or 24" paper *(green and/or white)*. The longer the paper, the more shamrocks you'll have. You can even fold two papers together.

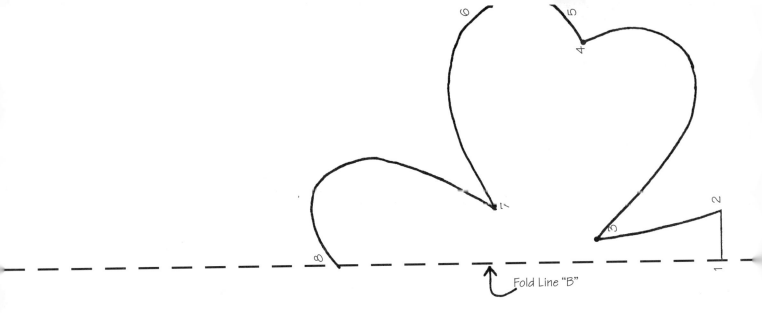

Fold Line "B"

Fold Line "A"

"A LUCKY CATCH"
Fold green paper at fold line "A"
Fold again at fold line "B"

6

The First Woman Doctor

How many of you know what you want to be when you grow up? Some people have always known what they want to do when they're grown up. But lots of people change their minds two or three times or more before they decide on a career. And sometimes a person just can't decide on what they should do.

That happened to a woman named Elizabeth about 150 years ago. She just could not put her finger on what she should do. *(Cut out hole, line #1. Stick finger through hole to emphasize this.)* She had lots of talents but just could not decide what to do.

One day one of her best friends became very sick. Elizabeth took care of her. Her friend said, "It is so great to have a woman taking care of me. If only women could be doctors. Elizabeth, I wish you were a doctor!"

Well—that gave Elizabeth an idea. Elizabeth could be a doctor—a very good one! She was smart and hard-working. Most importantly, she liked helping sick people and she was good at it.

Elizabeth worked for two years, studying and saving money so that she could go to medical school. Then she applied to medical schools all over the country. They all said, "No, a woman cannot be a doctor."

Elizabeth argued that she would be a very good doctor. But the directors of the medical schools said, "Women can't be doctors." Elizabeth asked, "Why not?" *(Cut out line #2 and show circle. Draw around the circle with your finger several times.)* They went round and round arguing about it.

Finally one director said that he would let the medical students vote to determine if a woman

should be allowed into their medical school. Thumbs up meant a yes vote and thumbs down meant a no vote. *(Show a thumbs up and a thumbs down sign as you do this. Then cut line #3. Show the paper thumb.)*

Just as a joke, all the students voted "Thumbs up!" *(Show the thumbs up sign that you just cut out.)* But they did not think she could really do it!

Elizabeth studied and worked hard all through medical school. She graduated at the top of her class. Elizabeth had achieved her dream of becoming a doctor.

As a doctor, she treated people who were too poor to pay for treatment. She helped other women, including her younger sister, become doctors, too.

Elizabeth Blackwell was the first woman doctor in America. *(Hold up her initials that you have just cut out.)* And these are her initials, "E" and "B." Elizabeth proved to the world that women can do anything they set their minds to do.

History shows us lots of women who have become professionals or done what they wanted to, despite enormous odds against them. These women have overcome many obstacles along the way. These women have achieved their dreams and made the world a better place to live. That's what we are celebrating during this month—Women's History Month.

Happy Women's History Month!

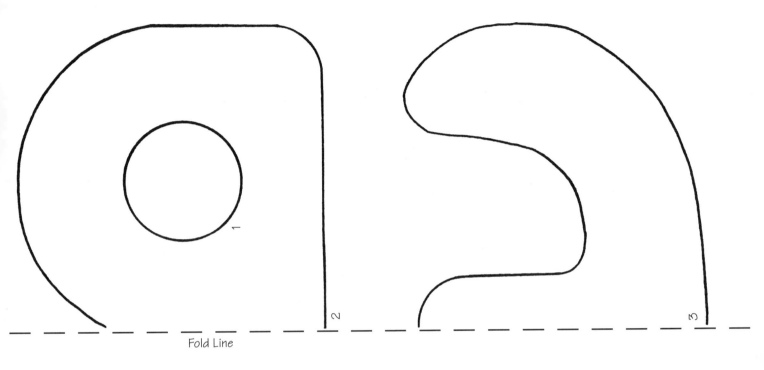

Fold Line

1

2

3

"THE FIRST WOMAN DOCTOR"

Fold colored paper in half at fold line

7

Earth Day Dolphins

Earth Day is a special time set aside to remind all of us that the Earth itself is a living thing and that we need to take care of it. Every animal, plant and person is an important part of our living Earth.

Sometimes a certain animal has a hard time surviving because that animal has difficulty finding food or a place to live. Sometimes people have hunted an animal until there are not many left. These animals are called "endangered." People make laws to protect these animals so that there might be more of them again.

One animal that has been placed on the endangered list is the dolphin. There are 45 different kinds of dolphins, and several them have been on the "endangered list."

Dolphins have been a favorite of people for many years. Dolphins always look like they're smiling, and they are friendly. They are also smart. Some scientists think that dolphins are the most intelligent animal after to people.

Dolphins associate with people in the ocean and in marine parks. There are many stories about dolphins and people. Today let's just mention a few of them.

Some dolphins become bow riders. This means that they catch a free ride on the bow or front wave that a ship makes. *(Cut from #1 to #2.)* A dolphin spreads out its flipper, keeps its body stiff and rides on the waves like a surfer. One famous dolphin named Pelorus Jack hitched rides with New Zealand ships for 20 years. Sailors considered him good luck.

Dolphins are also trained to help and to rescue people underwater. Dolphins can easily find their way around in the water by using the "melon" or big bump on their head. *(Cut from #2 to #3.)* They send out clicks and whistles from their melon and listen to the echoes of the sounds. This is called "echolocation."

One of the first "help and rescue" dolphins was named Tuffy. He wore a waterproof bag on his back. He could deliver tools and messages from scientists in boats to scientists working deep down on the ocean floor. Also, if a scientist got too far away from his boat, he could set off a special buzzer and Tuffy would come and find him. As his payment, Tuffy was always given a piece of fish. One time, a scientist forgot to give Tuffy his fish reward. Tuffy playfully bopped him on the head with his flipper before he swam off.

People have also taught dolphins to help protect swimmers against shark attacks. Dolphins swim up and down in the water looking for sharks that have come too close to a public swimming area. If they see a shark, they swim at once to a floating siren and push the button. *(Cut to #4.)* Then they swim back *(Cut from #5 to #6.)* to the shark and attack it if the shark has not been scared away by the siren's noise. Today, dolphins are on shark patrol at Florida and South African beaches.

Dolphins are very adaptable and easy to train. They can pull people through the water, fetch balls, throw rings and jump through hoops. One of their best tricks is jumping high out of the water. They can even do double jumps. *(Cut from #6 to #7 to #8 to #9.)* They enjoy it most when they have another dolphin friend so that the two dolphins can do tricks together.

One dolphin, Pauline, almost died after being put in a tank by herself. She did not eat or swim. She would not even swim to the top of the water to breathe. The scientists had to make a raft for her so she wouldn't drown. Finally, they put another dolphin into the tank. Pauline did not even see him because her eyes were closed, but she popped her eyes wide open when the new dolphin whistled to her. Instead of dying from loneliness, Pauline played water-tag with her new friend. *(Cut from #10 to #11 to #12.)*

You know, dolphins, like people, need each other! *(Unfold to show four dolphins.)*

Happy Earth Day!!

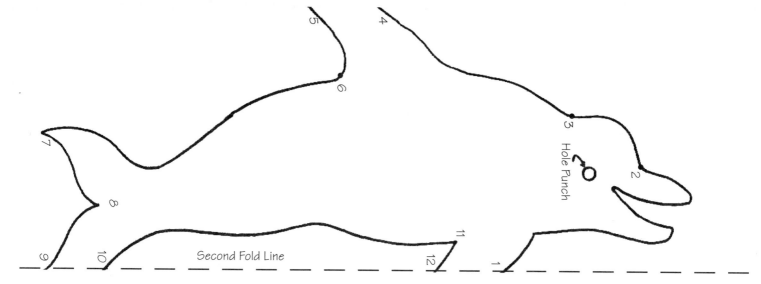

Second Fold Line

First Fold Line

"EARTH DAY — DOLPHINS"
Use blue, gray or white paper.
Larger paper works well also.

8

The Tooth-Picking Giants

A long time ago, before trees looked like they do today, the world was filled with giants—tooth-picking giants. *(Start cutting out brown tree, line #1.)* These giants were mean ones—mean giants with rotting teeth. That's because toothbrushes had not been invented yet. As you might guess, these giants weren't too smart, but they did use tooth-picks sometimes to clean their teeth.

You know that a toothpick this size (hold up toothpick) is not going to do much for a giant. These *(indicate toothpick again)* were not their toothpicks. Do you know what they used to clean their teeth?

Yes, tree branches! A giant would be taking a walk after lunch and feel something between his teeth. So he'd reach down and break off a branch from a tree and clean his teeth with it. But if his teeth still didn't feel just right, he'd throw that branch down, and break off another tree branch. If that one didn't work, he'd try another one. Why, a giant could use five or six tree branches in one toothpicking session! *(Tree should be half cut out.)*

After a while, all the branches on the trees were broken off and the trees were in danger of dying. They got together and decided they needed to do something to protect themselves from the mean tooth-picking giants. But what?

The trees couldn't think of a thing. They knew they had to hide from the mean tooth-picking giants. But how could they hide? Trees are rooted into the ground and can't move to a new place.

They decided to ask the Earth Spirit. They said, "Earth Spirit, those mean tooth-picking giants keep using us for toothpicks. *(Finish cutting out tree.)* Too many of our branches are getting broken off.

(Bend branches down.) We can't grow new branches fast enough and we are in danger of dying! Can you help us?"

Very early the next morning, a heavy fog settled over all the land, and was still there after breakfast. When the giants went out clean their teeth, they couldn't find the trees. They said to each other, "What are these clouds doing on the ground? And where are our toothpick trees?"

The trees were safe all that day; after breakfast, lunch and dinner. That night, the trees said to the Earth Spirit, "Thank you for keeping us safe today. But soon you will have to lift the fog. It can't be foggy all day, every day. That would not be fair to the other plants and animals. Whatever can be done?"

"Don't worry," said the Earth Spirit. "I have another idea." *(Put down brown tree and start cutting out green foliage, line #2.)*

That night the fog lifted. But in the morning little pieces of fog still remained on the trees. But these little pieces weren't white. They were *(pause)*… yes—green. Now the tooth-picking giants were totally confused.

When they came out after breakfast for their toothpicks, all they could see were green mounds and bumps and towers sticking up from the ground. "Where are our toothpick trees?" shouted all the giants. *(Finish cutting out foliage and place over branches.)*

For months, the tooth-picking giants searched everywhere for their toothpick trees. And then one day, a tooth-picking giant said, "You know, tomor-row, I'm going to look under those weird green things sticking out of the ground. Maybe that's where our toothpicks are hiding."

One of the trees heard the giant, and he was worried. He went to the Earth Spirit and said, "Earth Spirit, the tooth-picking giants are about to discover our branches hiding under these beautiful green leaves that you have given us. Tomorrow they are going to strip off all of our leaves, and we will be toothpicks again! Please, please help us!"

In the morning, there weren't any green things sticking up out of the ground. There were gold, red, purple and brown ones. This totally confused the giants again. *(Turn paper over to show orange side of foliage.)* The other thing that confused them was this! *(Put tree and leaves down and hold up a toothbrush.)* At the foot of every giant's bed was a …*(pause)* that's right—a toothbrush!

First the giants tried to clean their teeth with it like this. *(Pretend to clean your teeth with the wrong end of the toothbrush.)* But one of them accidentally put it in his mouth the wrong way. *(Now hold the toothbrush the correct way and pretend to brush your teeth.)* He ended up with clean teeth.

Then winter arrived, and it was time for the leaves to fall from the trees so that the trees could have a rest. *(Hold up branches only.)* But by that time, the tooth-picking giants were deeply in love with their toothbrushes. And they never again used tree branches as toothpicks!

Today we are celebrating trees. We call this day Arbor Day. It's a time for us to remember all the incredible things that trees do for us. What are some ways, besides toothpicks, that trees help us? *(Ask listeners to help you name ways such as shade, wood, beauty, homes for birds, animals, and insects, etc.)*

So we need to be nice to trees and not treat them like the tooth-picking giants did!

Happy Arbor Day!!

"TOOTH-PICKING GIANTS"
Fold brown paper in half lengthwise

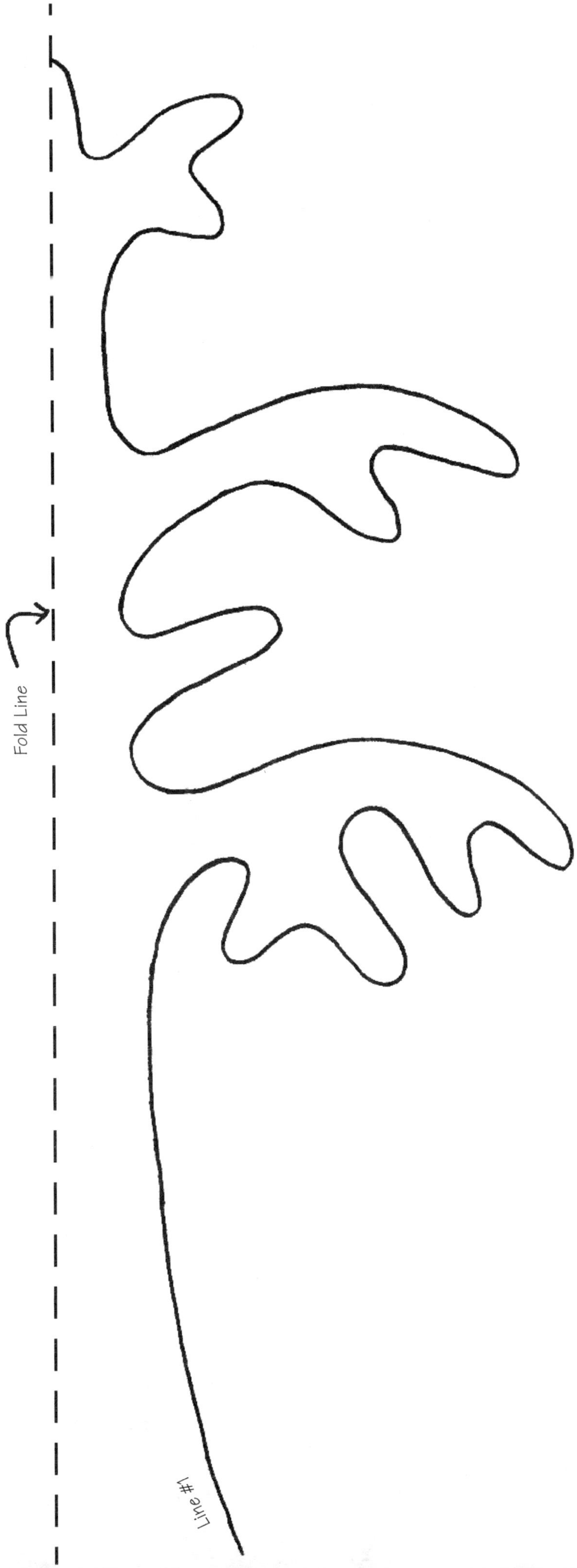

Fold Line

Line #1

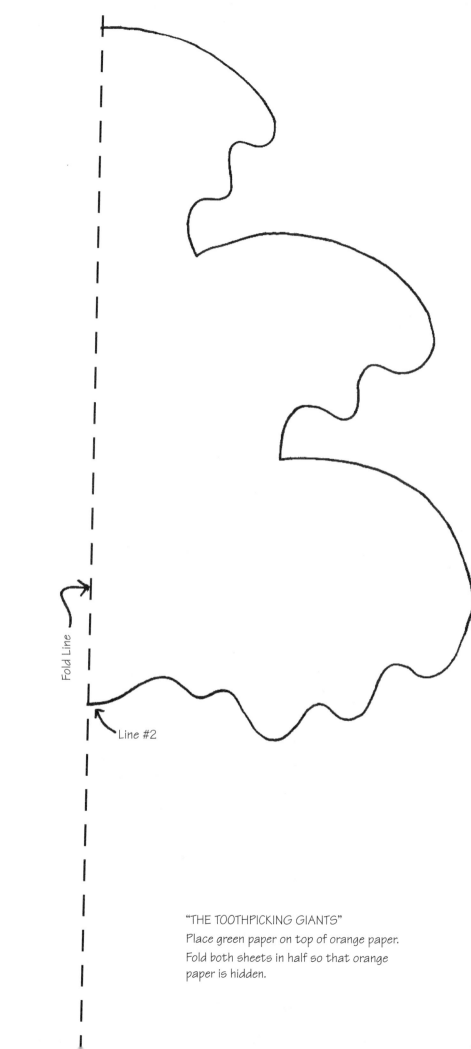

Fold Line

Line #2

"THE TOOTHPICKING GIANTS"
Place green paper on top of orange paper.
Fold both sheets in half so that orange
paper is hidden.

9

Cinco de Mayo

May 5th is a very special day for people in the United States and in Mexico. This day is called Cinco de Mayo, which means the fifth of May. It is celebrated with festivals, parades, parties, dances, sports events and music. Cinco de Mayo is celebrated especially in the southwestern United States and in Mexico. Why is Cinco de Mayo celebrated? This holiday is about a big battle that happened over 100 years ago, back in 1862 in Mexico. Here's the story—

Mexico owed a lot of money to three other countries—France, Spain and England. But it did not pay the money. The three countries wanted their money, and so they all decided to sail their ships across the ocean to Mexico to show that they were serious about wanting their money back. *(Cut from #1 to #2.)* They did not want to start any fights, and told everyone so.

The Mexican people talked to the French, English and Spanish people and agreed to pay back their money. So the British and Spanish ships turned around and sailed home. *(Cut from #2 to #3.)*

But the French ships did not go home. The French leaders had decided that they would like to conquer Mexico, or take it over. Instead of returning to France, 6000 French soldiers got off their ships and attacked two Mexican forts. *(Cut from #3 to #4.)* The French were certain that they were going to win Mexico easily. But the Mexican soldiers fought bravely and drove the French soldiers back to their ships. *(Cut from #4 to #5.)* The Mexicans had won the battle.

Later, however, the French soldiers did conquer Mexico. Their rule lasted for only three years. After that, Mexico once again became free and independent. *(Cut from #6 to #7.)*

Today, you can go to the city of Puebla, Mexico, which is where the famous Cinco de Mayo battle took place on May 5. You can see the graves of some of the French and Mexican soldiers who lost their lives in the battle. There is a big monument and a statue of a Mexican and a French soldier. *(Cut from #8 around to #9.)* They are shaking hands in friendship. *(**Open out paper to show both soldiers.**)* This statue shows that the countries of Mexico and France are friends now and are at peace with each other.

So, May 5, or Cinco de Mayo Day, is a celebration of a people who valued their freedom and wanted to live in peace with other countries. We can all learn from their story of bravery and desire for peace.

Happy Cinco de Mayo!

"CINCO DE MAYO"
Use blue or grey paper

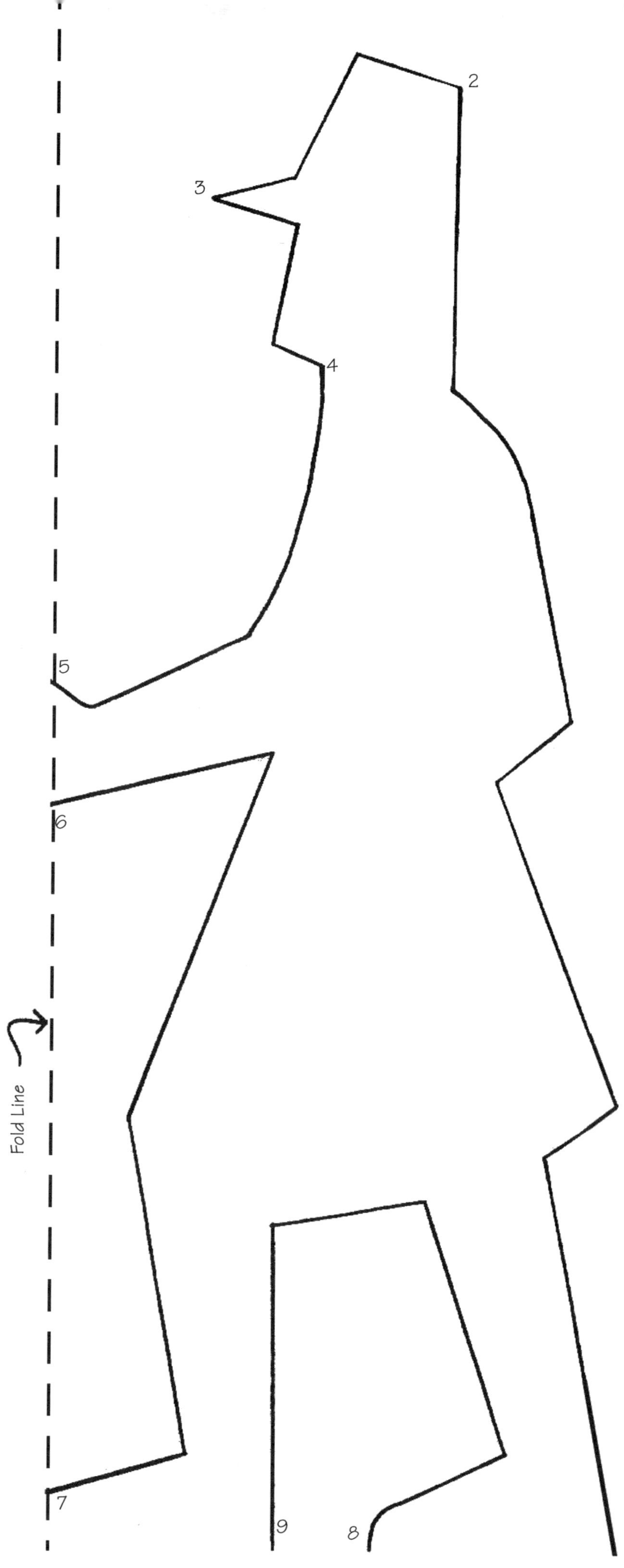

2

3

4

5

6

Fold Line

7

9   8

10

A New Flag

Julie rode her bike past her grandpa's house and looked closely at his front yard. It was then that she knew what she could give him for his birthday. His birthday was an important day. It was on May 31st, Memorial Day *(Or Nov 11th, Veteran's Day; or June 14th, Flag Day)*.

Grandpa was very proud to have his birthday on Memorial Day *(Veteran's Day, Flag Day)*, because he had been in World War II. "I served my country well," Grandpa always said.

Memorial Day is a day set aside to honor all of the soldiers who died in the wars of our country. For many years it was called "Decoration Day" because it is the custom to decorate the graves of the soldiers with flowers on this day.

or [The first Veteran's Day marked the end of World War I. It was November 11, 1918. That was the day the peace treaty, or armistice, was signed and the war ended. People all over the world celebrated. Now every year on November 11, sometimes called Armistice Day, we remember the signing of the peace treaty. More importantly we take time to remember all the men and women who fought in the wars. Some of the soldiers killed were not able to be identified. We did not know their names. So in 1920 a special tomb honoring these soldiers was erected in Arlington, Virginia. The tomb is in honor of all the unknown dead. Because we want everyone to know the tomb and the unknown soldiers are important to us, a soldier always stands guard at the Tomb of the Unknown Soldier.]

or [Flag Day, June 14th, is the day that the leaders of our country in 1777 adopted or approved of the flag as we know it today. They decided they liked the colors of red, white and blue. The white color stands for truth. The blue stands for justice or fairness to all and the red represents courage and bravery. The stripes *(seven red and six white)* represent each of the thirteen original colonies and each star represents a state in the United States. Today we have fifty states in the Union and fifty stars on the flag.]

Julie thought, "First, I'll need to earn some money. Let's see, what could I do? How about if I mow lawns? I'm good at that."

Julie walked up and down in her neighborhood, asking people if she could mow their lawn. *(Cut out strip #1.)* Some people said yes!

All that week Julie mowed lawns. She walked up and down behind her mower. *(Cut out strip #2.)* It was very hot, but she kept at it. *(Cut out strip #3.)*

One afternoon her friends asked her if she wanted to go get ice cream with them. Julie wanted to go but she had promised to get this lawn done by suppertime. *(Cut out strip #4.)* So she said no thanks.

By the end of the week and the last lawn, *(Cut out strip #5.)* Julie had enough money to buy her Grandpa that special present for his birthday.

She ran all the way to the store, gave her money to the clerk, and left with her gift in a white cardboard box. *(Cut out strip #6.)*

Julie ran all the way back to Grandpa's house. She burst in the door! "Happy Birthday, Grandpa! I bought a special present for you with money I earned all by myself!"

Grandpa smiled mightily and slowly took the box in his big hands. He opened it carefully *(Unfold paper and cut along line A on one side only. This frees up the flag stripes.)*

He pulled out a…. *(Pause and put red stripes on a piece of white paper. Hold so the stripes hang down.)* Flag! That's right!

"Oh Julie! What a great gift! You know it is something I really need. The flag out there on my pole now is looking a little tattered."

"Grandpa, I noticed that the other day when I was thinking of what to get for your birthday," said Julie.

"How ever did you earn the money for this beautiful flag?" asked Grandpa.

"Oh, I mowed lawns and the whole time I just kept thinking of how nice a new flag would look against the blue sky." *(Stick on the blue field — already cut out with a piece of tape on the back.)*

"Well, I'm proud to fly this flag. I was proud to serve America in the war and I'm proud to fly the flag of the United States of America." And he gave Julie a big hug!

Happy Memorial Day!
(Flag Day, Veteran's Day)

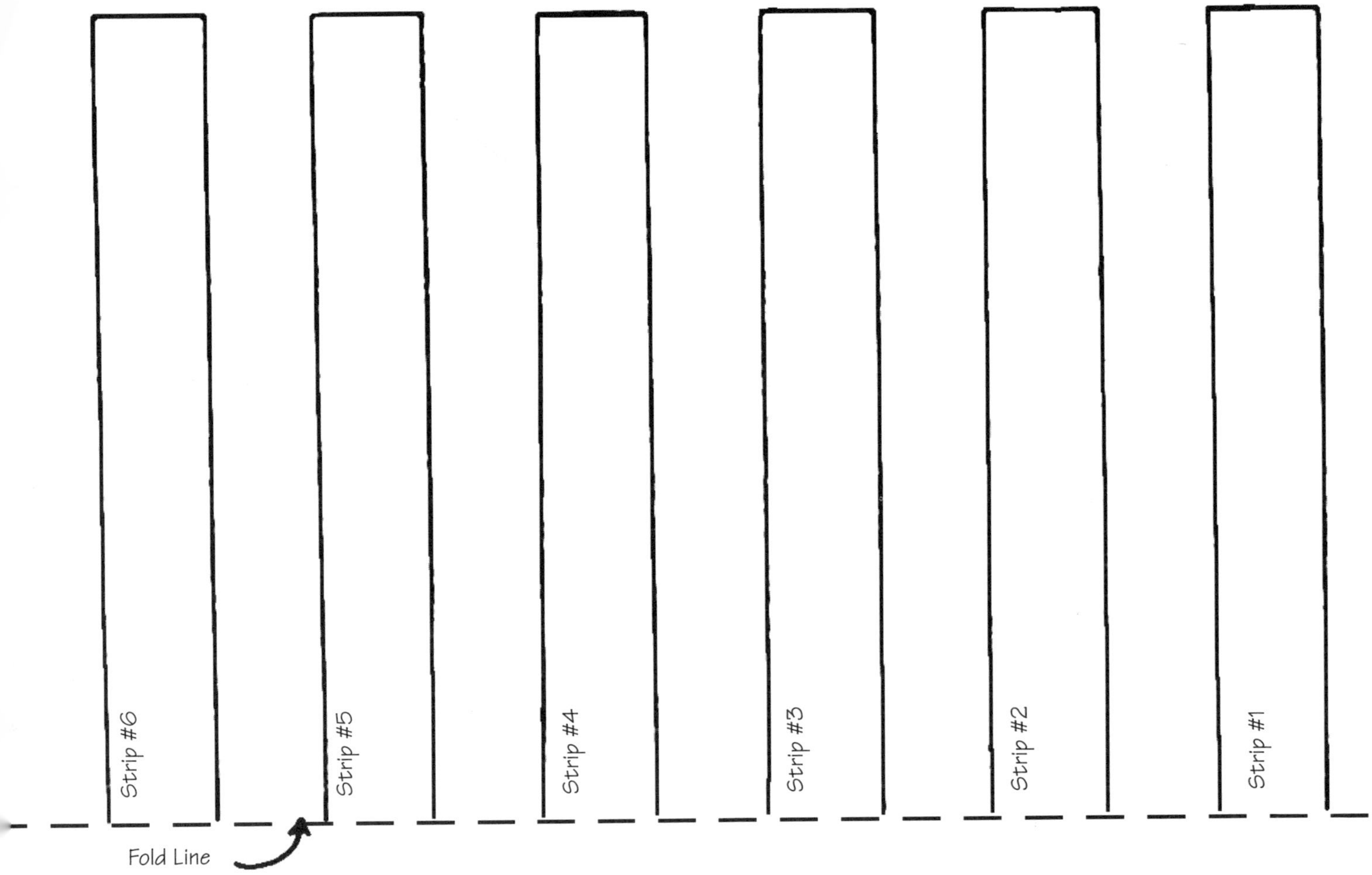

Strip #6

Strip #5

Strip #4

Strip #3

Strip #2

Strip #1

Fold Line

"A NEW FLAG"

Fold red paper in half at
fold line.

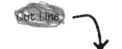

Cut Line

"A NEW FLAG"

Use blue paper

Cut out and place double
stick tape on back prior
to telling story.

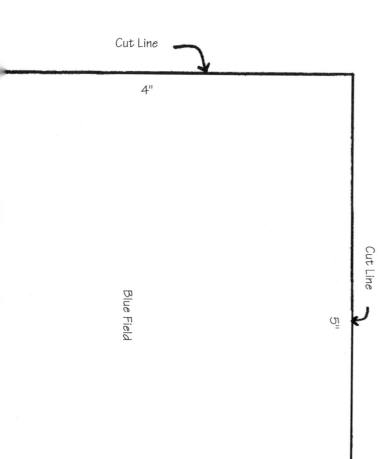

Cut Line

4"

Cut Line

5"

Blue Field

11
Not Just Another Tie

It was a week before Father's Day. David reached in his jeans pocket *(Cut out tie.)* and pulled out … what?—a piece of a tie!? *(Cut off bottom piece #1. Give to listener to hold.)* David said, "This is my Dad's tie, well—part of it, at least." He looked at the piece of paper pinned to it. "Look what it says 'I like how you helped me sort out the laundry this weekend.' This note is from Dad, I just know it."

The next day Natalie was opening her lunch box at school and found a piece of a tie under her cookie! Natalie said, "What is this piece of tie doing here in my lunch box? It has a note attached to it. "I like the way you helped me make the lunches for all of us today." *(Cut off piece #2 of tie. Give it to listener to hold.)*

That night Mikey went to brush his teeth. Taped to his toothbrush was a piece of tie and a note. Mikey said, "What is this doing on my tooth-brush? What is this note? It says, 'I like how you leave the sink clean after you brush your teeth.' Wow!" *(Cut off piece #3 of tie and give it to a listener to hold for you.)*

The next morning Cindy was opening the dish-washer when a piece of her dad's tie fell out. It also had a note attached to it. "What's this?" asked Cindy to herself. "This note says, 'I like how you help with the dishes.' Hmmmm." *(Give piece #4 to a listener to hold.)*

On Saturday morning the four kids got together to decide what they should get for their dad.

"Tomorrow is Father's Day," said Cindy. "What can we come up with for Dad?"

"I don't know," said Mikey. "I don't have any money."

"Neither do I," said David and Natalie at the same time.

"It'd be nice if we could think of something different this year. Seems like we always give him the same old thing." said Cindy.

"You mean give him a tie? for Father's Day? We always do that!" said Mikey.

"Mikey, that's exactly what we meant! Speaking of ties, this is so strange but I got a little piece of one of dad's old ties in my lunch box, with a note," said Natalie. And she pulled it out of her pocket.

"So did I!" said David. "Only not in my lunch box, but stuffed in my jeans pocket. Also, a note."

Mikey said, "I got one, a piece of tie, that is, on my toothbrush with a nice note."

"A piece of tie fell out of the dishwasher when it was my day to do the dishes. The note on it made my day!" said Cindy.

All four kids got out their pieces of ties. "Obviously, Dad doesn't want another tie this year. He's got so many, he's cutting them up and giving them away! But I liked the note," laughed David.

Natalie began to put the pieces of it back together. That gave Cindy an idea. *(Collect tie pieces #1 and #2 and tape together. Then collect #3 and tape to #1 and #2. Finally, collect #4 and tape it to the other pieces.)*

Cindy said, "I know what we can give Dad this Father's Day. It's a great idea and it won't cost us anything!" She whispered her idea to David, who passed on the secret to Mikey, who whispered it to Natalie.

"Yeah, great! I'll write the note!" said Natalie.

On Father's Day, the four children handed Dad a brightly wrapped tie box. Dad tried to look pleased as he said, "Oh, I see you got another tie for me!" Not too excitedly, he unwrapped it.

"Why this is my old tie! I see you guys put it back together for me. Nice tape job! I don't get it. I don't think I can wear it to work like this. Here's a note that says, 'We love you dad!'" Dad was puzzled.

"Dad," said David, "we were just finishing the message you gave us."

"Finishing the message?" asked Dad.

"Yeah, look at all the pieces of the tie put back together and see if you can figure it out." said Cindy.

"Think about it, Dad. The pieces put together make one tie," hinted Natalie.

"One whole tie!" hinted Mikey. Dad thought for a minute.

"OK, OK! I think I've got it. This week I cut up my tie and gave you all a piece. Now you are giving it back to me whole. I think this tie is like our family. Each piece of the tie is needed to make up the whole tie. Each piece is just as important as any other piece. The tie needs each piece to be complete. I think that means that though we are all separate individuals, together we make up a whole family. Like the tie, our family needs every member to be complete and everyone is important. That's right isn't it?"

"You got it!" said the four kids and they all gave each other one giant family hug.

"You know," laughed Dad, "this is the best Father's Day present ever! It's not just another tie!" *(Hold up tie again as you say last line.)*

Happy Father's Day!

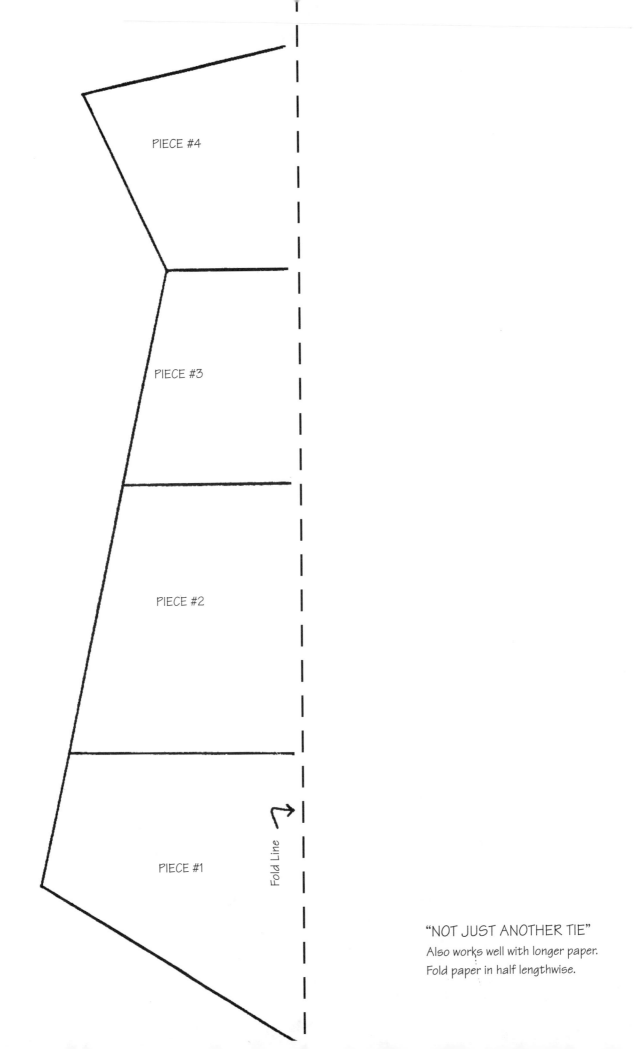

PIECE #4

PIECE #3

PIECE #2

Fold Line

PIECE #1

"NOT JUST ANOTHER TIE"
Also works well with longer paper.
Fold paper in half lengthwise.

12

The Liberty Bell

July 8, 1776 was a loud day! That's when most all of the church bells in America were rung to announce the adoption of the Declaration of Independence. The Declaration of Independence was an important document, or piece of paper, *(Cut out #1 to #2.)* that stated that the 13 American colonies were now their own country—the United States of America. We were no longer part of England.

There was one very special bell rung on that day. *(Slowly cut from #2 to #3.)* This bell was not new. In fact, this bell had been recycled—twice! The bell was originally made in England, and shipped to Philadelphia, Pennsylvania. It cost $300 and weighed about 2000 lbs. The bottom of the bell was 12 ft. around! So this was a big bell! *(Show bell.)*

People called this bell the Old State House Bell. This bell had special words, called an inscription, engraved in it. The message said,

PROCLAIM LIBERTY THROUGHOUT
ALL THE LAND UNTO ALL THE
INHABITANTS THEREOF

The bell arrived from England in 1752 and surprised everyone on the first ring—because it cracked! But it was such a long way to return the bell to England. Back then, the only way to get to England was by ship, and the trip took many weeks. So two men in Philadelphia were hired to make another bell. These men were John Pass and John Stowe.

First, they made a mold from the cracked bell. Then they heated up the bell to make it into liquid metal. *(Wad up bell.)* They added more copper to the liquid metal and poured it into the mold. When the bell was finished, *(Straighten and smooth out bell.)* they rang it. It sounded awful! Clunk! Clunk!

So John Pass and John Stowe tried again. First, they made a mold from the clunky-sounding bell. Then they heated up the bell to make it into liquid metal. *(Wad up bell again.)* When they had melted this second bell down, they added silver to the liquid metal. They thought that the extra silver would make the bell sound sweeter and not so clunky.

When this third bell was finished, it sounded better. *(Straighten and smooth out bell again.)* The bell makers did the best they could, but there were some pieces of lead that weren't entirely melted and so the surface was not smooth. *(Indicate your bell's surface. Then fold in half again.)*

The bell was hung in the State House in Pennsylvania. Because the inscription, or message, on the bell was about freedom it became a symbol of the American Revolution.

When the British were getting close to Philadelphia in 1777, everyone wanted the bell to be safe. So the bell was loaded onto a wagon to be taken to another town. The roads were very bumpy and the bell was dropped at least twice on its journey to safety. A small crack might have started then. *(Cut small crack, line #4. Unfold and show crack.)*

When the bell was returned to its home in Philadelphia, it was rung every year on July 4. We don't know exactly when the crack in the bell got wider, but it did. *(Cut line #5, reopen and display longer crack.)*

In 1846, someone tried to fix the bell by making the crack wider. But the bell still didn't sound any better.

Now the Liberty Bell is no longer rung. But it is tapped very gently on important occasions. For the last 20 years, the bell has been tapped every Fourth of July.

Today, you can see the Liberty Bell in a special glass building called the Liberty Pavilion in Philadelphia. Several million people see it every year. The Liberty Bell is known throughout the world as a symbol of American Freedom.

The Liberty Bell and the freedom that it stands for are important to Americans everywhere. We also have other symbols that stand for our freedom. Can you name some other symbols that represent freedom to us? *(eagle, flag, Uncle Sam, etc.)*

Today we remember how precious our freedom is to us. Happy Fourth of July! Let freedom ring!!

Happy Fourth of July!

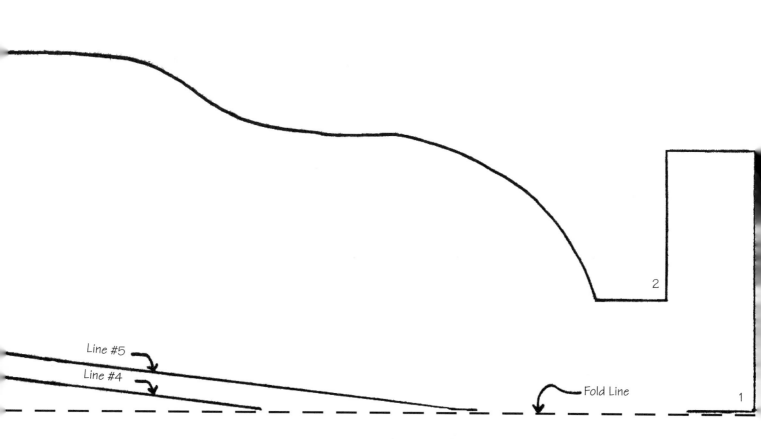

"THE LIBERTY BELL"
Fold paper in half
Use brown paper

2

Line #5

Line #4

Fold Line

1

13
I Don't Want to Go

It was the end of summer and Andy did not want to go back to school.

"Why?" his friend Liz asked.

"Well, school is so hard for me," explained Andy. "Sometimes I have to read." *(Fold paper in half. Hold it like a book.)*

"And sometimes you have to study shapes like squares. *(Fold paper in half again to make a square.)* And you have to do stuff with triangles." *(Set paper on your hand like a tent.)* I have trouble seeing how to do these things," said Andy.

Liz said, "Why don't you ask the teacher if you can sit closer to the front of the room? *(Cut on line #1.)* Then maybe school will be easier."

Andy said, "I guess I could walk up and ask her. *(Cut on line #2.)* But I want to feel like this about school. *(Show cut out smile.)* I don't want to feel like this, *(Show smile upside down.)* no matter where I'm sitting in the room."

"Actually, I'm sorry that summer is ending because I love to go swimming in the pool. *(Open cut out to show circle.)* Swimming is so much easier than trying to copy words off the chalkboard. Sometimes the words run together or I see two of everything," said Andy. "It makes it really tough. *(Open out cut out to show two circles.)* I just don't know what I'm going to do! How can school be easier for me?! *(Hold two circles up at eye level but away from face to begin to give the listeners an idea that Andy needs glasses.)* It is so hard to see; what I'm going to do!"

(Ask the listeners what Andy could do to make school easier. Give hints if necessary.)

Yes, Andy could get glasses! And that is just what he did. He got his new glasses right before school started. Now he could see so much better.

When the first day of school came, Andy actually found himself enjoying being back in school. His teacher was very nice to him and all the kids liked his new glasses. Best of all, his glasses helped him to do all the things that it had been so hard to do in the past.

I would like to welcome you all back to school. Happy Back to School Day! If you have a problem like Andy did in the story, please share it with me. That way we can work together to solve your problem.

Welcome Back to School!

"BACK TO SCHOOL—
    I DON'T WANT TO GO"

Fold paper in half at Line "A,"
then fold in quarters at Line "B."

Fold Line "B"

Fold Line "A"

Line 1

Line 2

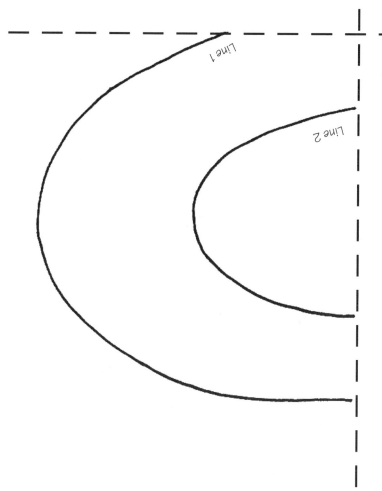

14

Two Packages

Grandparents Day in September was always a special time for Breck and Judy. That weekend they always went to see their grandparents who lived far away. Every year before that special weekend came, Breck and Judy always got a package in the mail. They each got their own package.

Some years, Breck would get his package from Grandma and Judy's would be from Grandpa. Sometimes, it was the other way around and Judy's package would be from Grandma and Breck's would be from Grandpa. Inside the packages there was always just one item. That item was a clue about what Judy and Breck were going to do when they arrived at Grandma and Grandpa's house.

This year, as usual, two packages arrived at Judy's and Breck's house. One package was very long and narrow. *(Cut box out, line #1.)* The other package was smaller but also long and narrow. *(Cut box out, line #2.)* The bigger one was addressed to Judy and the smaller one to Breck.

Judy tore off the wrappings fast. *(Quickly cut out the fishing poles, line #3.)* and inside there were two.... *(pause)* Yes—fishing poles! A card tucked inside said, "See you soon. Love, Grandma." Judy was puzzled, "I didn't know Grandma liked to fish or even knew how!"

Breck opened his small, thin package. *(Cut on line #4.)* Inside were there were two......*(pause)* Yes—sewing needles! A card tucked inside said, "See you soon! Love, Grandpa!" Breck was puzzled. "I didn't think Grandpa liked sew or even knew how!"

Breck and Judy looked at each other and laughed! Judy said, "I'm going fishing with Grandma!"

Breck said, "I'm sewing a quilt with Grandpa!"

As soon as Breck and Judy got off the plane, they saw Grandpa and Grandma waiting for them. After the hello hugs, Breck and Judy looked at each other and started laughing. Both Grandma and Grandpa said, "What's so funny?"

Breck and Judy said, "We are excited about what we get to do with you this weekend. We got our packages." Breck pulled out the box from his backpack and carefully unwrapped the two sewing needles and held them up. Judy pulled the fishing poles out of her suitcase and held them up.

Judy said, "You know both things are very similar. They are both long and narrow. They are both made out of metal and have holes in the end of them so that you can put the line or thread in." *(Hold up the fishing poles in one hand and the needles in the other hand.)*

Breck laughed, "I just have one question. How easy is it to catch a fish with a sewing needle?"

Judy laughed, "And I want to know how you sew with this fishing pole? Pretty big stitches, huh?"

Grandma and Grandpa were quiet for a second and then burst out laughing. "Oh, I get it! Breck's package was the sewing needle. And Judy's was the fishing pole!" said Grandpa. "We accidentally switched the tags."

Grandma said, "But that gives me a good idea! Let's all go fishing and you two guys can teach us girls how to fish. And then we'll go home, and we gals will show you how to sew!"

Breck, Judy and Grandpa agreed that this was a good idea. So they all went fishing and then they all sewed! *(Hold up poles and needles.)*

Many people have grandparents who live far away and so they do not get to see them very often. That makes it really special when grandparents come to visit us or we get to go and visit them. Grandparents know how to do lots of things, like fishing or sewing, and perhaps they show us how to do them. Sometimes if we don't have a grandparent close by or our grandparent has died, we can become friends with an older neighbor or someone else from our family, like an aunt or uncle. Grandparent's Day is celebrated in September and it is a time to remember our grandparents, and other older loved ones, no matter where they are, or who they are. Maybe you can send a card or make a telephone call to your grandma or grandpa or other favorite relative and wish them a —

Happy Grandparents Day!

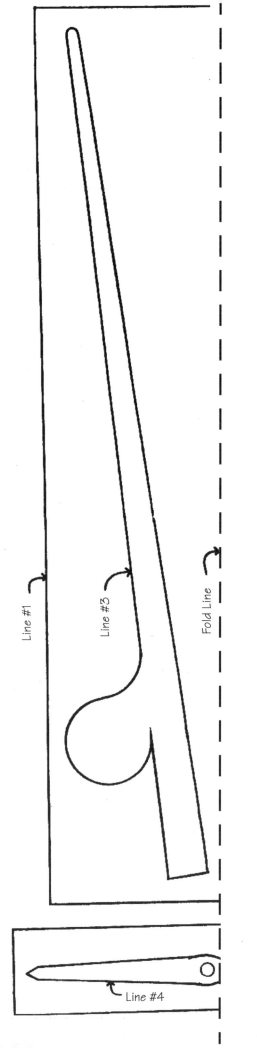

"TWO PACKAGES"

Fishing poles & needles

Fold paper lengthwise

Larger paper works well

Punch eye of needle before starting story

Line #1

Line #3

Fold Line

Line #4

15

Cabin Girl

Have you ever heard the legend that says Christopher Columbus wasn't the first member of his crew to land in the New World but the second? The story says that the cabin boy Patrick McGuire jumped off the rowboat and laid his coat down on the shore so that Columbus wouldn't get his feet wet.

Well, I'm here to tell you that legend is only partly true. It was really cabin girl—*Patricia* McGuire—me. *(Point to yourself.)*

I loved to draw, especially ships. Everyday that I could get away, I went down to the wharf with my drawing paper stuffed up under my shirt.

Oh, I couldn't go down to the docks just like that. *(Snap fingers.)* No, I had to get ready. It wasn't easy. I had to completely change clothes before sneaking out. I put on my brother's pants and his old shirt and jacket. I put my hair under a cap. Fortunately my hair was short to begin with so it wasn't too much of a problem. Then I hid my drawing charcoals and paper under the shirt. *(Cut from #1 to #2.)*

Down at the wharf, I'd make sketches of ships. In my disguise, no one paid much attention to me, even though I went there a lot. I guess they just got used to seeing me there. It was fun to watch the ships coming and going, and the sailors loading and unloading them.

Sometimes ships leaving didn't have enough sailors to make up the crew. Then if an unlucky sailor happened by at the wrong time, he could be "volunteered" to be a crew member.

That's what happened to me. For months, the port of Palos was extra busy. The Queen of Spain, Isabella, had commissioned a very smart but unusual sea captain named Christopher Columbus to sail three ships westward across the Atlantic. No one had ever tried to reach the Indies by going west. But Columbus thought the Earth was round. An unusual idea, that was!

Anyway, at the last minute, one of Columbus's sailors "volunteered" me to be the cabin boy. I said I didn't want to go. I said my mother would worry. I even said I was a girl! I whipped off my cap to prove it, but they all laughed and said lots of boys needed haircuts these days.

It was August 3, 1492, and there I was on a ship with only my sketch paper and charcoals and my poor mother not knowing where I was. Ship life was hard. Oh, I didn't have to do much work, just fetch and carry things. The food was terrible and the ship was cramped and smelly. The sailors worried all the time about sea monsters and demons rising up to destroy them.

As the captain's personal servant, I had special privileges and Columbus himself watched out for me. He even showed me how he used his compass to determine which way was north.

Just when we had all given up hope of ever finding land—we had not seen any for almost two months—there it was! And Christopher Columbus told me to get our Spanish flag *(Cut from #2 to #3 —second sail)* and come with him and a few other sailors in the rowboat. It was exciting but scary!

When we rowed up to the beach, I leaned over to spread out my cloak for him, so he wouldn't get his feet wet, you know. But I leaned out too far and fell in the water. You might say I landed first in the New World! Only we didn't know then that it was a whole new world. Everyone thought it was the edge of Asia. *(Cut from #3 to #4—third sail)*

We returned to Spain three months later. We brought back bits of gold, new foods, brightly colored birds and six of the people we found in the new land. We called them Indians. There was a parade and we were all heroes.

As soon as I could I slipped away and ran home. I had had a terrible, wonderful adventure and I was so glad to be home. And by the way, no one ever found out that the cabin boy was really a cabin girl!

Christopher Columbus was a great adventurer and a brave man. He made four voyages in all. But you know what the best thing I think Columbus did? Oh, it's true, he did discover new lands and help start new colonies. But what he learned on his trips made life easier for many people in the Old World. Sailors on ships now used hammocks to sleep in. *(Cut from #4 to #5—boat. Trace finger on boat to show curve of hammock. Then open up to show ship.)* Before that they just slept anywhere on the hard wooden deck. People also began using canoes. These are both ideas borrowed from the Native American people whom we found there. Most important was the food. Columbus brought back corn, beans, tomatoes, pineapple, green peppers, strawberries, avocados, and papayas. These were all foods that Spain and the rest of Europe didn't have before his trips.

Columbus gave us inspiration to try out our new ideas and stick with them. He had the courage to spend years working, and working hard, toward his dream. He had the courage to sail where others dared not go. His story *and my story* is truly an exciting adventure story!

Happy Columbus Day!

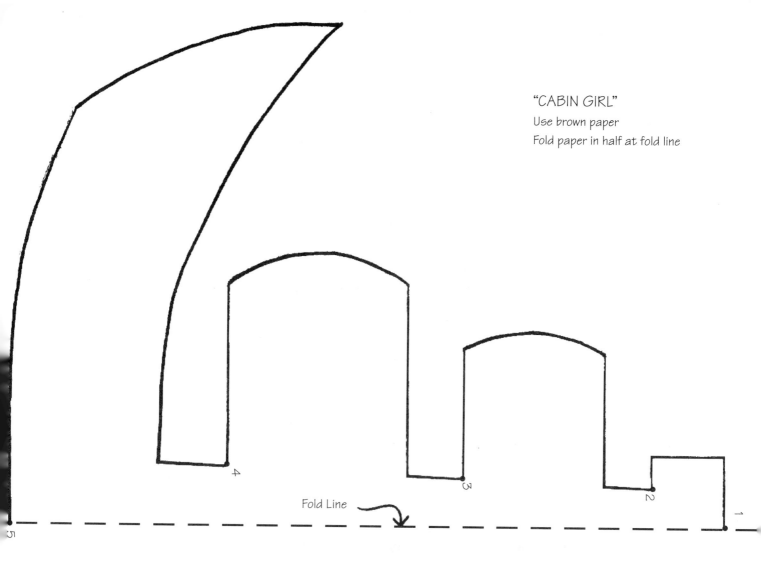

"CABIN GIRL"

Use brown paper

Fold paper in half at fold line

4

3

2

1

5

Fold Line

16

A Revolutionary Ghost Story

"I sure hope that George Washington stops here on his way home from his hunting trip. I want to show him the trick with our new heating machine," said Roger Stanley. Roger lived with his family in a beautiful and stately mansion built on a hilltop overlooking the Potomac River. It was only a few miles from Mount Vernon, George Washington's home. *(Cut from #1 around to #2.)*

Sure enough, George Washington stopped to visit at the Stanley's home. George was very interested in the "heating machine." Today, we would call it a stove. It was six feet tall, made of iron and covered with scrolls and curlicues. This was to make it look like a fancy cupboard. *(Cut from #3 around to #4.)* "Does is really work better than our fireplaces?" asked George Washington.

"Well, not really. It either gets too hot or stays cold. But someday, I hope that we can replace fireplaces with machines that bring heat to every room in a house, even though that room doesn't have a fireplace. Meanwhile, this heating machine has been a fun toy for Roger!" laughed Mr. Stanley.

"What do you mean?" asked George Washington.

"Roger, why don't you show him?" said Mr. Stanley.

Roger quickly opened the door of the stove. *(Cut line A. Unfold once. Cut line B. Open paper up completely and fold door open.)* Roger squeezed himself into the stove. Then he put his face up to the pipe which led to the chimney of the fireplace. He groaned loudly. "Oooooh!" he yelled. Almost at once the stove answered back with an even stranger sounding "Oooooh!" Roger and the stove groaned back and forth to each other several times, filling the house with ghostly noises! George Washington was amused.

Roger did not see George Washington again for a long time because the American colonies had begun the fight for freedom from England. Washington left his home to lead the colonists in their fight for freedom. Roger's father also left to fight in General Washington's army. Right before Mr. Stanley left, Roger helped his father bury their family jewels and other treasures in the garden behind their house. That was to keep them safe if enemy soldiers burned the Stanley's home.

Roger was extremely worried that the English would sail up the Potomac River to his home and then go on to Mount Vernon, General Washington's home. So he went down to the river every day to watch for English ships.

And then it happened! Roger went with his mother and sisters to visit a neighbor. That was the day that the English soldiers did come. Fortunately, Roger had decided to return home early and had left his family to continue their visit.

As Roger turned his horse into the lane leading up to his house, he saw red-coated soldiers standing on his porch.

Quickly, Roger got off his horse, leaving it behind a stand of trees, and walked quietly around to the back of the house. He silently stepped into his house, trying to think of a plan. But there were soldiers coming into the house! Roger had just enough time to hide himself in the heating machine! *(Open and close the door again.)*

When the soldiers came closer, Roger could hear them talking about burning his house!

"No!" Roger protested loudly without even thinking! The stove echoed back, "Noooo, noooo, noooo…"

"What was that?!" asked one soldier. "It sounded like a ghost!"

"You're hearing things! There are no ghosts in here. Let's just burn the house, dig for the family treasures out back in the garden and leave. No one will even know who did it, and we'll be rich. Say, isn't that general's home around here somewhere, too?" answered the other soldier.

Now Roger knew what he had to do to save his home and General Washington's. Roger moaned and groaned better than he had ever done before. The stove groaned back—better than it had ever done before! It sounded like the entire house was filled with ghosts!

Both the soldiers rushed out of the house. They ran for their boats and shoved off. Would they go on to Mount Vernon and burn General Washington's home or would they return to their fleet? Roger followed them and watched as they turned their rowboats toward their fleet.

Whew! Both homes were safe! Roger and his ghostly stove had served their new country well. And that's the story of Roger and his ghostly stove! **(Indicate stove again.)**

Happy Halloween!!

(This story can also be used to celebrate George Washington's Birthday, Feb. 22.)

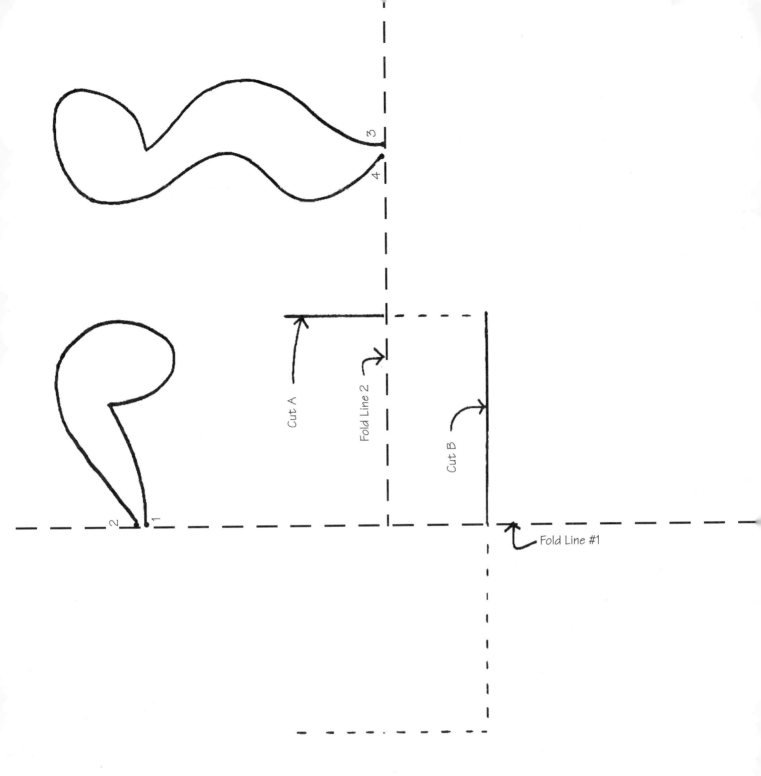

3

4

Cut A

Fold Line 2

Cut B

2 1

Fold Line #1

"A REVOLUTIONARY GHOST STORY"
Fold black paper in half at Fold Line #1
Fold again at Fold Line #2

17

Turkey Feathers

Turkeys have been around for a long time. *(Raise your hand if you're planning on having a big turkey meal this month.)* The turkey meat that you eat today comes from turkeys raised on turkey farms. Turkeys weigh between 10 and 24 pounds.

But before we had turkey farms, people hunted wild turkeys for food. They looked for the turkeys in low branches of trees where turkeys like to sleep. Hunters also looked on the ground where turkeys build their nests and look for nuts, insects and berries to eat. It's hard to catch wild turkeys, so people started raising them for food. But they didn't always!

Turkeys used to be the fattest, flyingest birds you ever did see. But something happened to change all that—here's the story!

A long time ago, turkeys looked a lot different than they do today. Oh, they had feet. *(Cut foot, #1 to #2, then #3 to #4.)* But their wings looked like this. *(Cut wing from #4 to #5.)* And here is the head. *(Cut from #5 to #6. Open out to show turkey.)*

Now these turkey wings; they were made of one big feather. All the other birds had small individual feathers but turkeys had one big feather on each side. *(Indicate each wing.)* Turkeys are quite big birds but with wings this big they could fly high and low. *("Fly" your turkey high and low.)*

The turkeys just loved flying around so that all the other birds would notice them. One day while a turkey was flapping around, he didn't notice that one of his enemies, the eagle, was nearby. Just as the turkey was flying backwards, *("Fly" turkey backwards.)* the eagle attacked him! Fortunately the turkey swerved just in time and the eagle ended up only biting the turkey's wings. *(Fold turkey*

together and cut out notch A. Then open out again.)

That was a close call! "Oh well," said the turkey, "I've still got my big feathers. I just can't fly quite as high."

Not long after that the turkey was flying along doing his double flips. *("Fly" turkey lower and make him do a flip or two.)* A man shot at him. The arrow missed him but got his feathers again! *(Fold turkey together and cut out notch B. Then re-open turkey.)*

"Not again!" said the turkey. "This is bad, very bad. I can still fly, but now only just barely above the ground. Well, at least my wings are still better than all the other birds' wings. Think I'll try my turns." *(Fly turkey lower, turning him this way and then that way.)*

But the turkey was too low and a fox who was hiding in a bush jumped up and bit his wing. *(Fold together and cut notch C. Then re-open.)*

Now the turkey did not have great big wings anymore, but individual feathers just like every other bird.

"Oh well," said the turkey. "I don't have the biggest wings anymore and I can't fly high. But my feathers are still the prettiest of all!" And he strutted around all day on the ground.

That turkey was so busy strutting that he didn't notice a woman looking at him. That woman saw him and his pretty feathers. "I'd like to have some of those beautiful feathers for myself. Since they look so pretty on the turkey, they'll look great on me." She caught the turkey (when he was busy strutting) and put him in her barnyard, and took his feathers. *(Fold turkey together and cut off all his feathers, line #7. Re-open.)* Then the turkey looked like this. *(Indicate turkey again.)*

You know, that fat turkey strutted around her barnyard without any feathers. *("Strut" the turkey back and forth.)* That gave the woman's husband an idea. "I wonder if that turkey tastes as good as he looks!"

And that's how we ended up with turkey for Thanksgiving and holiday dinners, and lots of turkey sandwiches, and turkey hot dogs, and turkey bacon, and turkey bologna, and turkey salami, and turkey, turkey, turkey…

Happy Thanksgiving!!!!

"TURKEY FEATHERS"
Fold orange paper in half at fold line
Punch eye before starting (optional)

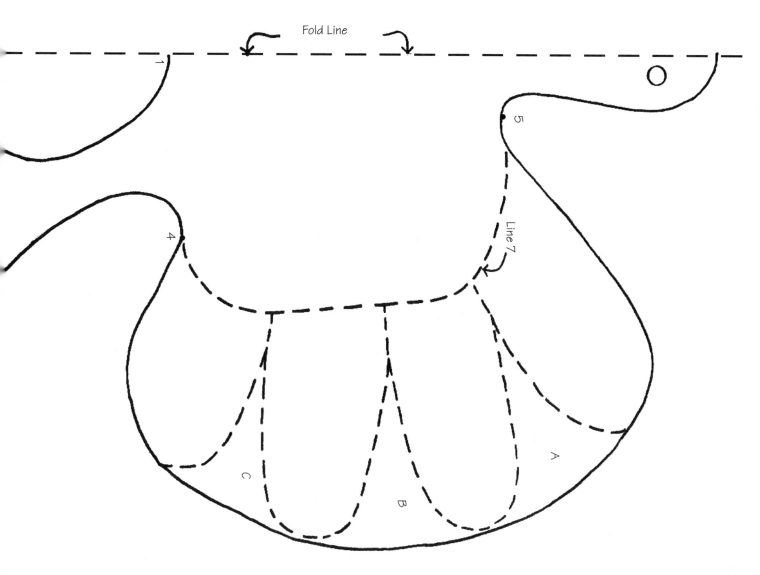

Fold Line

1

O

5

Line 7

4

A

B

C

18
Cookie Cutters

Ben sat on the floor, waiting for his mom to come down from the attic with his favorite toy. But instead of carrying the big box into the living room, she brought in an old battered suitcase.

"Mom, you said you were going up to get special things for Hanukkah. That's not the box that my favorite dreidel is packed in."

"I know I did son, but then I saw this old suitcase of my grandma's. I guess I had forgotten that I had it up there. I wanted to take a look at the special things of hers that I've saved. I think we should start a new 'old tradition.'"

Mom carefully opened up the suitcase. Inside was an old shawl. She lifted it out gently.

"What's a new 'old tradition'? And what's wrapped up in that old shawl?" asked Ben. *(Cut on line #1.)*

Mom set the shawl down on the table and began to unfold it. First there was a Star of David. Ben knew it represented his faith. *(Open and hold up Star.)*

"Was that Grandma's? It looks more like a cookie cutter than a Hanukkah decoration." said Ben.

"Well, you know this was a cookie cutter, but it never cut out any cookies," explained Mom.

"Oh, maybe that's because it's so old and tarnished," said Ben.

Mom pulled out the next thing from the folds of the shawl. "Here is the dreidel." *(Refold the Star of David and cut on line #2.)*

"Oh, it's a cookie cutter too!" said Ben. *(Open out dreidel.)*

"Here is the last cookie cutter. It's supposed to look like a jug," *(Refold and cut on line #3.)* said Mom.

"A jug?" asked Ben. *(Open out to show jug.)*

"Yes, remember when our Jewish ancestors cleaned up and rededicated their Jerusalem temple to God? They found only one jug of sealed, pure oil to burn. It was supposed to last only one night but instead, the oil in that jug burned for eight days! It was a miracle! This shape reminds us of that jug." *(Hold up jug again.)*

Ben asked, "Why did Grandma have cookie cutters of these things? Why didn't you ever use them? She must have used them a lot. They sure are old and tarnished. Wait, you said they never cut out any cookies! I don't understand."

"Ben, I'm going to tell you the story of these cookie cutters. *(Hold up all three outlines.)* It is an important one.

Many years ago, when my mom, your grandma, was a young girl, the Jewish people in her small town were persecuted. *(That means they were treated badly.)* Most people in her town were not Jewish, and a few of these people made life terrible for your grandmother and her family. Sometimes these people would throw rocks at their windows, or yell things at them. Many times when the Jewish people left to worship at the synagogue, their homes were broken into and their valuables stolen. My grandmother, your great-grandmother, did not want this to happen to them. They all talked about how they could hide their valuables. Then David, my mom's older brother, your great-uncle, had a great idea about how to keep their silver coins, spoons, forks and knives from being stolen. David was a jeweler, and he took all their silver and melted it down. He made it into something that no thief would think of stealing."

"Wow, what was that, Mom?"

"Actually, he made several things—common kitchen items, that no one would pay any attention to. What do you think they were?" *(Hold up three cut-outs. Give listeners a chance to guess.)*

"Yes, you are right. He melted the silver into cookie-cutter shapes. These cookie cutters! Of course, no one ever made cookies with them. The very next Hanukkah they moved to a bigger city, one which had a large Jewish community. They were happier there, living among their friends and they did not have to worry so much about being persecuted. But they did not turn all their silver back into silverware. Instead, every Hanukkah, they hung these three silver cookie cutters on the wall in a place of honor."

Ben said, "I think we should do that too, Mom. Is there any way we can shine them up a bit?"

"Yes. A little silver polish will make them bright again. Would you like to polish them, Ben?"

And that's how Ben and his family started a new "old tradition" in his family. They decided to continue a family tradition that had been in their family a long time. Every Hanukkah, they told the story of the cookie cutters and remembered their family's history. The Jewish people have a rich and exciting history, filled with many stories of bravery and change.

Happy Hanukkah!!!

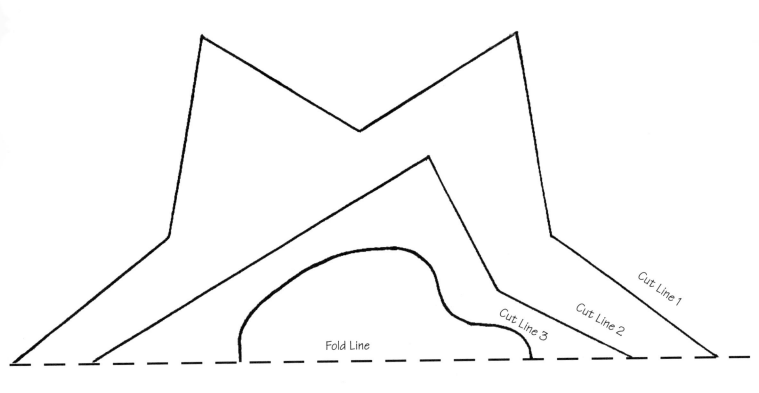

Cut Line 1

Cut Line 2

Cut Line 3

Fold Line

"COOKIE CUTTERS"
Fold paper in half at fold line.
Use silver or gray paper.

19

The Christmas Angel & The First Christmas Tree

It was the Christmas season, Weston's favorite time of year. Everyone was getting ready for Christmas. People were wrapping presents, baking cookies, singing songs and walking around with big smiles on their faces.

This year Weston wanted to give his mom an extra special present—one that no one had ever given her before. When Weston had asked his mom what he could give her, she had answered, "Thank you sweetheart, but you don't have to get me anything."

Weston decided right then that he was going to get his mom, maybe even his whole family, the best Christmas present ever! He didn't know what yet, but it would be something—something special.

That afternoon, after school had been dismissed for Christmas vacation, Weston decided to take a "thinking" walk in the woods behind his house. As he walked through the snow, *(Cut from #1 to #2.)* he thought and thought about what his gift could be.

After a while, he came to a little clearing in the woods. Right in the middle of the clearing stood a little tree, all by itself. It looked rather funny standing there all alone and Weston walked over to it. He looked at it. You know, there was something different about this tree, but he couldn't quite figure out what it was. So he looked closer.

It had snow on it, like the other trees in the forest, but this snow looked different. It seemed to sparkle more. It had berries on it, like the other trees, but these berries were different. Instead of just red berries, this tree also had green, blue, silver and even a few gold ones!

As Weston looked at the tree he decided that it was the most beautiful tree he had ever seen—it was so different from the other trees in the woods. This tree seemed to have a special glow about it.

Then Weston got an idea—he would give this tree to his family for Christmas. His mother would love its beauty and its glow!

The woods were getting dark and he realized that it was almost suppertime. Excitedly, Weston rushed back home on the trail that he had blazed to his new discovery. *(Cut from #2 to #3.)*

The next morning Weston got dressed quickly. As he ran downstairs, his mother asked, "Weston, do you want to go with all of us to Grandma's house? We won't be gone long."

"Not right now, Mom. Tell Grandma I'll be along soon." As soon as they were gone, Weston grabbed his ax from the barn and ran through the woods. *(Cut from to #3 to #4.)* Would he be able to find the clearing again? Would the tree still be there? Would it look the same as it did yesterday?

Yes, there was the clearing and there was the tree. Yes, this small tree still had that special magic, that special glow about it. Yes, this was the special present to give his mother and his whole family.

Weston swung his ax to chop down the tree. But wait! If he chopped it down, that would kill the tree. Somehow that didn't seem quite right. So how could he get the tree home?

Yes, he could dig up the tree, roots and all, and put it in a big pot and then take it home. That's what Weston decided to do. He ran back to the barn, *(Cut from #4 to #5.)* put away his ax and got out a shovel and the biggest pot he could find.

59

Weston rushed back to the clearing, *(Cut from #5 to #6.)* carefully dug all around the tree, and put it in the pot. He hauled the tree home *(Cut from #6 to #7.)* and set it on the front porch. He rang the doorbell but no one came to the door. Then he remembered that they had all gone to visit his grandmother.

"Well, I'll just put my tree in the living room. *(Cut from #7 to #8.)* That way when they come in they will see my wonderful gift." Weston set the tree down and took a good look at it. But there was something wrong! Terribly wrong! The tree didn't look the same! The snow was melting and the branches didn't look sparkly anymore. The berries were falling off. Somehow this just looked like a plain old tree. His Christmas gift wasn't anything special. Weston sat down and began to cry.

And the Christmas Angel heard him! The Christmas Angel—you know—the one who flies around every Christmas looking for a special miracle to do! She flew down to have a look. *(Cut from #8 to #9.)* She hovered outside the window. *(Cut from #9 to #10).* She could see Weston in front of his tree crying, but why was he crying? She looked closer at the tree. *(Show tree.)* There were puddles of water and little berries on the floor around it. The tree looked as sad as Weston.

The Angel listened to what Weston was thinking. This is what she heard. "Maybe if I just explain about how beautiful the tree was, my family can use their imaginations to see it like it really was. If I tell them about how the snow glistened on the branches and how it made the tree so sparkly, maybe they can imagine it."

Weston shut his eyes tightly and saw the tree as it had been. That gave the Christmas Angel an idea. The imagination and love of this little boy was so great that she wanted to help him. Could she make his tree look like it had before? She concentrated very hard. She made the branches sparkle again, and she made the berries larger and hung them back on the branches. And the last thing she did was put an angel, one that looked just like herself, at the very top of the tree. Yes, the tree was just as wonderful as Weston had remembered. *(Turn tree around to show decorated side.)*

Just then his mother walked into the room. "Look! A tree! In our house. It is so beautiful! Look at the lights, the colored balls! And look what's at the top of the tree! She's so beautiful!"

Weston opened his eyes. He walked over to the tree and touched it. "It looks so real."

It wasn't snow that made the tree sparkly—it was lights, tinsel, and garland. Those weren't colored berries—they were glass balls of different colors. Then he looked up toward the top of the tree. There had been nothing there when he had brought the tree inside, but now there was an angel perched on the highest branch. And it seemed to Weston that she was smiling right at him.

"Weston, is this from you? What a beautiful gift!" His mother beamed and hugged him. "This gift is a miracle! However in the world did you do it?" his mom looked so happy.

"I don't know, Mom. I guess it is a miracle," replied Weston as he gazed at the little Angel.

Weston was right. The tree was a miracle—the Christmas Angel's miracle.

And you know, friends and neighbors from all around came to see the glistening tree in Weston's house. They liked it so much that they decided to put up trees just like it in their own homes the very next Christmas, with lights, tinsel, garland and colored balls.

And that's why we have Christmas trees in our homes today—because of Weston and the Christmas Angel's miracle.

Before telling this story: Trace the tree onto both sides of green paper, lining up the inside with the outside. At the end of this story, you will open up the cut-out tree to show the decorated tree inside. So you will need to "decorate" the inside of the tree.

For the "lights, tinsel, and garland"—use glitter sprinkled on glue lines and dots. Or draw white and yellow chalk lines and dots.

For the "balls"—use colored stick'em dots, colored dots, colored chalk or markers, or cut out circles from colored construction paper and glue on.

For the "Angel"—use pattern from this book and cut out and glue entire angel on the tree at the top, or use a sticker. Add facial features and decorate as desired.

During the cutting, be careful to hold the tree so that no one can see the decorated side until you turn it around.

"THE CHRISTMAS ANGEL &
   THE FIRST CHRISTMAS TREE"
Fold paper lengthwise at fold line

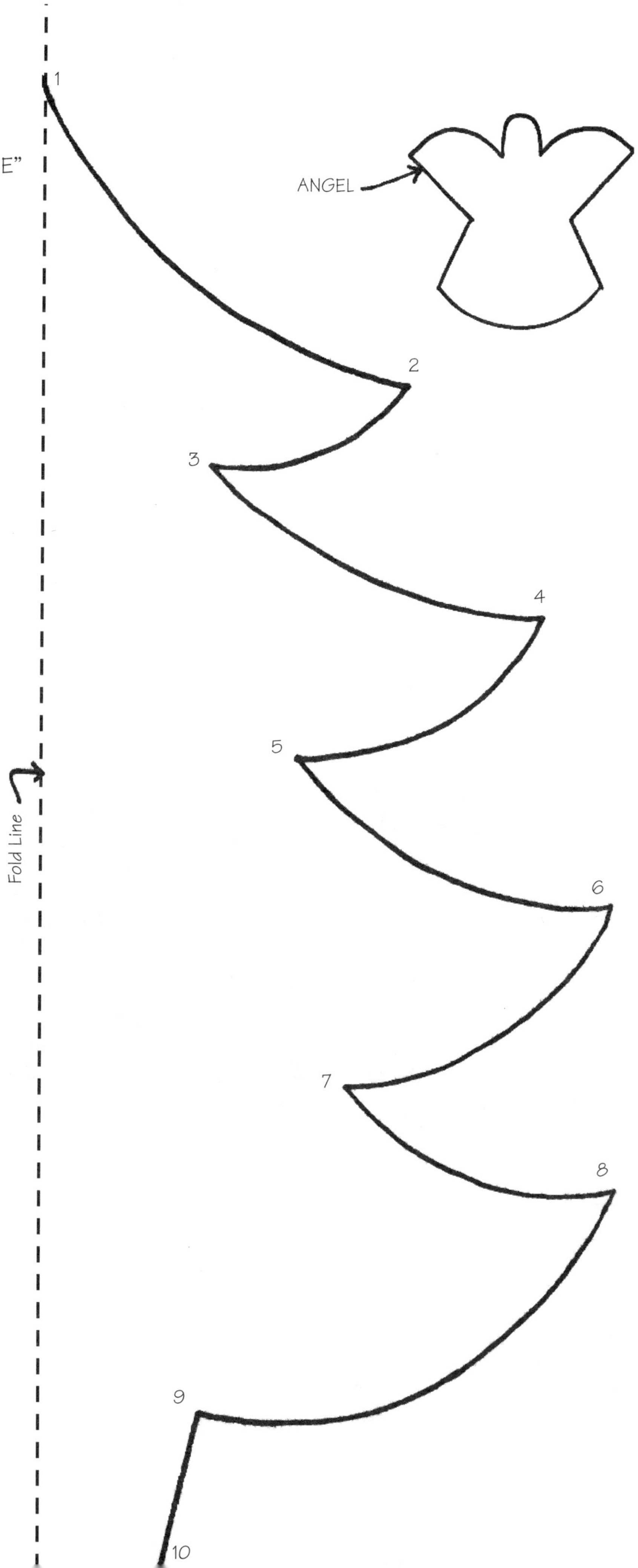

ANGEL

Fold Line

1
2
3
4
5
6
7
8
9
10

20
Kwanzaa

Everyone knows that there are several major holidays at the end of the year, Hanukkah, Christmas and New Year's. Now more and more people are finding out that there is another holiday celebrated at this time. This holiday is called Kwanzaa *(KWAN-zaa)*. It begins the day after Christmas *(Dec 26th)* and ends on New Year's Day. It is an African American holiday based on African agricultural celebrations. Kwanzaa celebrates seven principles, and each principle has its own day of celebration. These principles are goals that all of us can believe in and strive toward.

On the first day of Kwanzaa, Umoja *(U-MO-JA)*, which means unity, is celebrated. We light a candle and remember people like Harriet Tubman who helped slaves in the Southern United States escape to freedom in the North. *(Cut out base of candle holder and candle #1.)* She believed in Umoja, or the unity principle.

The second day of Kwanzaa stands for Kujichagulia *(KU-JI-CHA-GU-LIA)*, which means self-determination. This means standing up for ourselves, and working hard to achieve our goals. Marian Anderson was a person who worked hard toward her goal of singing. She had a wonderful voice and wanted to give concerts for people. She became a very famous singer. Marion Anderson also worked for world peace as a representative to the United Nations. On the second night of Kwanzaa, we light the candle of Kujichagulia, or determination. *(Cut out candle #2.)*

The third principle of Kwanzaa is Ujima *(U-JI-MA)*, which means collective work and responsibility. Charles Drew was an American doctor who organized many blood bank programs. Healthy people give blood so that someone who is sick can get well. Charles Drew's work shows us that we can work together for each other. *(Cut out candle #3.)* The candle of Ujima is lit on the third night.

The fourth principle of Kwanzaa is Ujama *(U-JA-MA)*. Ujama means cooperative economics, or earning a living by helping each other and working together. George Washington Carver was born a slave on a farm in Missouri. Then slavery was abolished in 1865, so he was free. Carver worked his way through college and became interested in helping farmers improve their methods of farming. He worked with the peanut plant and peanuts and discovered many ways people can use them. He also worked very hard his entire life to improve relations between blacks and whites. He knew Ujama, or working together, would help everyone. *(Cut out candle #4.)* On the fourth night of Kwanzaa, we celebrate Ujama or cooperative economics.

On the fifth night of Kwanzaa, we light the candle of purpose, or Nia *(N-IA)*. Booker T. Washington was a man with a purpose. All his life he worked to help other African Americans learn practical work skills. He started a school that first met in an old church. The school taught people how to be carpenters, farmers, mechanics and teachers. Today Booker T. Washington's school is a famous college called Tuskegee University. Booker T. Washington believed in his Nia (or purpose) of helping people. *(Cut out candle #5.)*

The sixth night of Kwanzaa is called Kuumba *(KU-UM-BA)*, meaning creativity. We all have areas in which we are creative. Ernst Just was a biologist who studied sea animals. He used his creativity to take a different look at how animals such as starfish, sea urchins, and clams reproduce.

(Cut out candle #6.) Kuumba, or creativity is an important part of everyone's life.

The seventh and last night of Kwanzaa stands for faith, or Imana *(I-MA-NI)*. Colin Powell is a person with Imani or faith. He has served two terms as Chairman of the Joint Chiefs of Staff. That means that he is in charge of all the men and women in the Armed Forces. These men and women are dedicated to bringing peace to the world. Colin Powell has faith that our world can be a peaceful, safe place to live. *(Cut out last candle, #7.)*

Just as the Kinara *(KI-NA-RA)*, or candle holder, holds all the candles together, so can we work together and always strive for cooperation. *(Finish cutting out candle holder.)* The African Americans that we have talked about all worked hard to make this world a better place for all of us. Each one of them had their special contribution to make to the world, and it was something that the world needed very much. Every single one of us here has our own unique contribution to make to the world. It is important for us to remember that.

The Swahili word for pulling together is Harambee *(HA-RAM-BEE)*. Can you say that? Ha-ram-bee.

This year, between Christmas and New Year's Day, you can remember the African American holiday of Kwanzaa and the seven principles. *(Point to each candle as you review the principles.)*

The principles are:
1. UMOJA—unity
2. KUJICHAGULIA—self determination
3. UJIMA—collective work
4. UJAMA—cooperative economics
5. NIA—purpose
6. KUUMBA—creativity
7. IMANI—faith

And on New Year's Day you can wish everyone *Harambee* seven times!

(Point to each candle again and say HARAM-BEE seven times)

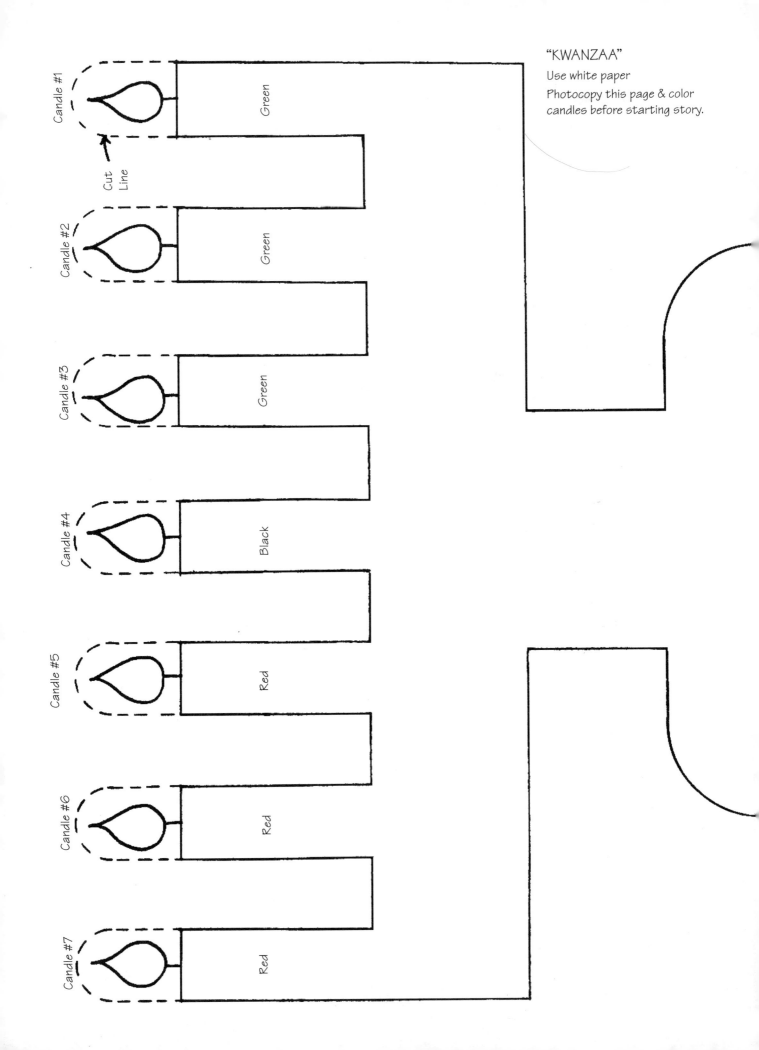

Candle #1

Cut
Line

Green

Candle #2

Green

Candle #3

Green

Candle #4

Black

Candle #5

Red

Candle #6

Red

Candle #7

Red

"KWANZAA"

Use white paper

Photocopy this page & color candles before starting story.